WOMEN IN
LAW ENFORCEMENT

WOMEN IN LAW ENFORCEMENT

By

PETER HORNE

Assistant Professor
Department of Criminal Justice
Meramec Community College
St. Louis, Missouri

CHARLES C THOMAS • PUBLISHER
Springfield • Illinois • U.S.A.

Published and Distributed Throughout the World by
CHARLES C THOMAS · PUBLISHER
BANNERSTONE HOUSE
301-327 East Lawrence Avenue, Springfield, Illinois, U.S.A.

© *1975 by* CHARLES C THOMAS · PUBLISHER

ISBN 0-398-03305-6

Library of Congress Catalog Card Number: 74-11493

With THOMAS BOOKS *careful attention is given to all details of*
manufacturing and design. It is the Publisher's desire to present books
that are satisfactory as to their physical qualities and artistic possibilities
and appropriate for their particular use. THOMAS BOOKS *will be true*
to those laws of quality that assure a good name and good will.

Printed in the United States of America
Y-2

Library of Congress Cataloging in Publication Data

Horne, Peter.
  Women in law enforcement.

  1. Policewomen—United States. 2. Policewomen.
I. Title
HV8138.H66   363.2′2   74-11493
ISBN 0-398-03305-6

To Anne and Stacy

ACKNOWLEDGMENTS

I WOULD LIKE TO THANK the people who aided me in the completion of this book. Without the many policewomen in Southern California and St. Louis who talked freely and candidly with me, there would have been no book. My only regret is that I cannot thank them individually here, but their anonymity should be preserved. My parents, Bernard and Katherine Horne, performed some very valuable "leg work" for me. A secretary, Elaine Piech, was a vital aid. Diane Carson, a friend and English Professor at Meramec Community College, assisted me with the many intricacies of the English language. Dr. Ronald K. Lingle, Assistant Dean at Meramec Community College, aided me greatly with proofreading. Dr. Lewis J. Sherman of the University of Missouri at St. Louis gave me some valuable thoughts concerning women in policing and my thanks to him and his wife, Marion, for permission to use their very fine "Bibliography on Policewomen: 1945-1972." My thanks to Dr. Richard O. Hankey of Linn-Benton Community College for his assistance. I would also like to thank Anne for all her help and encouragement.

PH

CONTENTS

WOMEN IN
LAW ENFORCEMENT

CHAPTER 1

←INTRODUCTION

L AW ENFORCEMENT in the United States is under intense pressure in the 1970's. At no other time in history has society placed such an immense burden on law enforcement. The stresses are aimed at the police from external, as well as internal, sources. Externally, citizens are demanding more effective and efficient law enforcement. Internally, police officers are demanding increased benefits in the form of wages, hours, working conditions and, in many cases, management and policy-making decisions within the department.

The police administrator of today faces a rapidly changing society. Thus the traditional methodology of police work must change in order to accommodate new societal values and mores. For effective policing in the 1970's will not have the same meaning as effective policing in the 1960's, or any other decade for that matter.

In response to these altered factors, police departments are rapidly embracing the technology of today through the use of computers and other modern techniques of crime control. This embracing of modern concepts, though, must carry over into police agencies' personnel field as well. In fact, skilled and qualified police officers are a necessity if police departments hope to modernize and meet the varied demands being placed upon them both today and in the future.

Thus, the focus of this book will be to examine one of the most sorely neglected areas of personnel usage—the policewoman.

The purposes of this book are to:

1. examine the usage of policewomen in other countries,
2. examine the current use of policewomen in America,
3. explore the positive and negative arguments concerning the use of women in law enforcement, and

    4. recommend a course of action for the future usage of policewomen.

Several reasons warrant an examination of this subject. One finds a scarcity of literature on policewomen.[1] Some literature exists on the early history of the American policewomen through the 1930's, but following that there is only a small amount of pertinent material relating to the subject. Only within the last two or three years has any current research or written material been published concerning women in law enforcement.* Writings about policewomen in other countries prove even more difficult to obtain. It is almost as if the policewoman never existed or, if she did, she was considered an oddity and not worthy of an in-depth examination of her role.

This lack of contemporary writings and research about policewomen, coupled with an awareness of women's restricted role in American law enforcement, prompted this book.

Law enforcement is striving to become a profession, but it will become one only when it makes effective use of all its personnel. Since public pressure demands that police administrators get maximum use of their personnel, the utilization of policewomen may help to achieve this. This book is directed not only to law enforcement administrators and officers but also to concerned citizens of both sexes who want to see our police agencies operating more effectively and efficiently.

DEFINITION OF TERMS

General patrol. This term refers to the basic police technique of using uniformed officers to prevent and suppress crime in assigned areas and is generally performed today by officers operating from marked patrol vehicles.

Large-sized police departments. This term indicates a police department with over 150 sworn police officers.

Medium-sized police departments. This term refers to a police department with over 20 but less than 150 sworn police officers.

Nonsworn personnel. Nonsworn personnel include all civilian employees who have not taken an oath of office and do not have the police power of arrest.

Officer. An officer is one of the personnel of a police department who has taken an oath of office and has police power to arrest.

*See current and comprehensive bibliography.

Small-sized police departments. This term refers to a police department with less than twenty sworn police officers.

Specific patrol. Specific patrol involves police officers, usually in plain clothes, concentrating on certain crimes and problem areas, such as juvenile, sex crimes, burglaries and others, and operating from unmarked vehicles.

Sworn personnel. Sworn personnel are all officers with authorized police powers of arrest.

METHODOLOGY

Throughout this book, comments from various female officers have been used. Many of these comments are excerpts from interviews conducted by the author with policewomen from various Los Angeles County police agencies in the spring of 1971.* Additional and current comments have also been gathered through conversations between the author and policewomen from several St. Louis County police departments. The respondents were promised anonymity to facilitate a more candid response, and for this reason, throughout the book, the respondents' statements are followed by a code number.

These policewomen are representative only of themselves. Statistical manipulation of the responses of only thirty nonrandomly selected policewomen would be spurious.

The interviewed policewomen are from eleven different-sized police departments and all have varied backgrounds, rank, job usage and working milieus. Excerpts from these interviews are incorporated in the book so that individual policewomen could express themselves concerning the proper role of women in law enforcement. From these opinions, though, a clear and definite picture of women in police work emerges which will be of benefit in evaluating the use of policewomen today and in the future.

REFERENCES

1. Gary R. Perlstein, "Female Police: The Need for Research," *Police*, XV, 1 (September-October 1970), 62-63.

*Research conducted for Master of Science Thesis "Role of Women in Law Enforcement," California State University, Los Angeles, June, 1972.

CHAPTER 2

HISTORICAL AND PRESENT ROLE OF POLICEWOMEN IN FOREIGN COUNTRIES

T HE USE OF POLICEWOMEN in foreign countries progressed in slow stages, just as it did for their American counterpart. First, departments tried the tentative employment of a few women, often untrained and without police powers, on selected duties. Next came recognition of their value in dealing with women and children whenever women and children came in contact with law enforcement agencies. Then, only at this point, were women given police training and police powers. Literature on foreign policewomen is as scarce as that on American policewomen; however, the author, with the aid of correspondence with foreign police administrators, has attempted to present as much information as possible.

Great Britain

Established democracies in Western Europe tend to make considerable use of women in their police functions. The pioneer in this area has been Great Britain, where policewomen have played a vital part in police work for almost sixty years. In 1907, the first woman "police aide," a Miss Macdougal, was appointed to take statements and interrogate female victims of sexual assaults for the London Criminal Intelligence Division; however, she had no arrest powers. Then in 1916, Clara Holmes became the first policewoman in the Carlisle Police Department in northern England. After her training with male recruits in London, she was assigned preventive police work involving women and children. Women's groups and civic groups supported the drive to get women into police work at this time. As World War I left England short of manpower, women received the opportunity to prove themselves in law enforcement. Throughout the war, women patrols helped keep activities of women and children under surveillance. Although paid from police funds, they did not possess the power of arrest, and they had to call male officers before an arrest could be made.

On November 21, 1918, because of the effective work done by the women's patrols, the Metropolitan Police of London designated the first official body of policewomen. Called the Division of Women Police Patrols, it was composed of one female superintendent, one female assistant superintendent, ten female sergeants and 100 women patrols. Primarily this division dealt with wayward girls, sex offenses, prostitution, white slave traffic, female prisoners and all juvenile cases. But still, the English government considered women social workers and not police, and the women police patrols lacked the power of arrest and eligibility for pensions.[1]

There was considerable resistance to women doing police work during this time. In Great Britain, there was concerted opposition to policewomen by the all-male police federations of England, Wales and Scotland.[2] The federations felt that the entry of women into police work would militate against the welfare of the policeman. Also, while the federations believed in a need for some preventive work, they did not feel that the women engaged in it should have police powers. In 1922, the forces against policewomen found their official "voice" in the government-sponsored Geddes Report which called for the abolition of policewomen in order to save money because policemen could perform all necessary police tasks. Soon, the number of women patrols in London was cut to twenty as their yearly contracts came to an end. Women's groups led by Lady Astor asked the International Association of Policewomen, which was based in America, for help in saving the principle of women officers in police departments.[3] The association's president, Lieutenant Mina Van Winkle, went to England and helped to fight the antipolicewomen forces. In 1923, the Home Secretary of Great Britain created the position of woman constable with full police power to arrest, and by 1924, there were fifty women constables on the Metropolitan Police (greater London police).*

In 1931 the Home Secretary issued the Women Police Regulations which gave women conditions of service similar to men, as well as the same training and the same promotion and instruction courses. In the thirties, the Metropolitan Women Police force was increased to 200. Miss D. O. Pete was appointed to the Commissioner's staff with special responsibility for women (until then women police had been under the supervision of male officers), and under her leadership Women Police became an accepted branch of the Metropolitan Police Force.[4]

During the Second World War women police had to contend not only with law enforcement duties but also with air raids, escorting enemy aliens and performing duty in detention centers on the Isle of Man. In 1946, Metropolitan Policewomen undertook special missions in British-occupied Germany and Berlin to reestablish German policewomen sections. Thus British policewomen have been used in various parts of the British Empire in different capacities over the years.

Although the early years were difficult for British policewomen, the intervening period of time has proved their worth. By 1971, female positions constituted approximately 4,400 of the 101,000 authorized police positions in Great Britain or about 4 percent of the total strength of the police forces. Furthermore, these positions extend to the administrative ranks. Women Commanders, Chief Superintendents, Superintendents, Chief Inspectors and Inspectors exist in a representative number of positions on not only the Metropolitan Police but also other police forces in England, Wales and Scotland as well. Of the eleven Inspectors of Constabulary in Great Britain, two are females. It should be noted that the Inspectors of Constabulary hold a very important position in the British police system. Each local police force throughout Great Britain receives a fifty percent grant toward its expenses each year from the Home Secretary who is responsible for the operation of the police on the national

*An interesting book about this period is an autobiography by Mary S. Allen, Commandant of the Woman's Auxiliary Service, entitled *The Pioneer Policewoman.* (London, Chatto and Winders, 1925, Republished New York City, 1973, A. M. S. Press Inc.)

government level. The grant is given to a police department (only 67 departments in Great Britain), provided that the Inspectors of Constabulary issue a certificate of efficiency for it during their formal annual inspection tour.[5] Even the Police Federation (a police union of sorts) has three of the 21 seats on its Joint Control Committee held by policewomen.

The selection criteria differ somewhat for male and female police applicants. The minimum height for males is 5'8" and for women 5'4". The maximum age for joining for a woman is 35, that for a man, 30 years. While men and women train together in the same sixteen-week police academy, women do receive some additional training in work connected with juveniles. One of the negative aspects of the policewoman's role in Great Britain is that she receives only 95 percent of the male officer's pay. The reasoning behind the pay differential is that women were given supposedly less arduous assignments than males in deference to their sex; however, legislation has now been passed which will give them equal pay with men starting in January 1974. Another negative difference between men and women officers existed until February 1973. As a separate section within the department, women had their own rank structure with certain posts set aside for women holding rank. They did not compete directly with men for promotion. So while males and females took the same promotion examinations, policewomen had to wait for openings in their own, limited, promotional structure. Now there is no separate rank structure for women nor any bar to them holding any post.[6]

With the closing of the separate women's police section on the Metropolitan Police Force, the full integration of policewomen has become official. While British policewomen have always performed the traditional "female side" of police work, i.e. searching female prisoners, dealing with prostitutes, juvenile matters, interviewing female rape victims, today and in recent years they have become involved in the whole spectrum of police work. She is used on uniformed general patrol, specific patrols, plainclothes detective functions, planning and research, training and in every and any aspect of police work that male officers perform. There are no restrictions on what a woman police officer may do or how high she can rise in rank on the force. Furthermore, policewomen are fully accepted by the public. The attitude of British police administrators is now one of full acceptance of policewomen, and they feel that each police officer, female or male, should have the opportunity to be employed on any duty which is suited to her or his individual capabilities.[7]

Women are also used in two quasi-police functions in Great Britain. Almost 2,000 women special constables volunteer to perform police duties without pay in their spare time.[8] They are very similar to their American counterpart, the police reserves or auxiliary police. There are also traffic wardens in Great Britain who handle much of the traffic control functions, freeing police officers for crime prevention and detection. These traffic wardens check parking violations, direct moving traffic, act as school crossing guards and perform other traffic related tasks under the direction of the chief constable of the area in which they are employed. Over 50 percent of the approximately 5,000 traffic wardens are women.[9]

West Germany

Stuttgart, Germany, became the first city in the world to employ an officially titled policewoman in 1903. Since then Germany has used policewomen, except in the Hitler era. After World War II, West Germany used policewomen to aid democratization and fill minimum personnel needs of police agencies. As in many defeated countries after a war, the male population was severely diminished. The government took policewomen out of uniform, and now they dress mostly in civilian attire. Policewomen are not used in much crime suppressive work, such as decoy or criminal police tasks, but deal mostly in preventive work with women and juveniles. In fact policewomen handle almost all police matters involving women and have exclusive jurisdiction over boys and girls under fourteen years of age. German police officials make it their practice to recruit only women who have had some experience in work of a "social" nature, such as teaching, nursing, social work and so on.[10] Police officials require women to go to a one-year training school to learn general educational subjects as well as subjects relating to women and juveniles.

The German policewoman role is changing, though. In 1970 in North Rhineland-Westphalia, the largest of West Germany's ten states, policewomen were assigned to general detective work after proper training. Berlin now uses the "traffic warden" concept as in Great Britain and employs women in these positions, too.[11]

Poland

The use of policewomen in Poland has a short but proud and innovative history. After World War I, when Poland was once again an independent country (for the first time since 1795), the women police force was started in 1925. They were organized as part of the state police force, and their duties were to combat prostitution, to curtail traffic in women and children and to cooperate with social organizations engaged in the prevention of juvenile delinquency. The first thirty policewomen and all thereafter received three months of training at the police academy along with male officers. The policewomen carried guns and had full police authority. The policewoman was expected to perform all police functions, as well as to bring social methods, in which she had special training, to the prevention of delinquency and to the rehabilitation of juveniles. By 1939, over 300 policewomen in fifteen cities operated under the centralized command of a female chief commandant. Then, with the outbreak of World War II, many policewomen fought and died alongside males in their defense of Poland.[12] Today, there are still policewomen in Poland, although it is difficult to obtain accurate information about this Communist country's police agency.

France

France provides an excellent example of almost nonusage of policewomen. In answer to a 1925 questionnaire, French town mayors stated that women were not on their police forces because women were meant to be homemakers and mothers and should not be employed where there is physical danger.[13] As of 1969, in all of France, there were only fifty-nine policewomen with their baccalaureates who held the title of "social assistant" but had little to do with everyday police work.[14]

One woman who has broken out of this narrow and restrictive role for French policewomen is Daniéle Thiery. Initially she worked on an undercover drug assignment for six months. Her principal problem was that neither colleagues nor suspects took her seriously. But that all changed as she made good arrests to prove herself. She is presently the head of a ten-man drug squad in Lyon.[15]

Japan

Japan is one country that should be examined because of its current progressive use of policewomen. The birth of the policewoman's movement started in 1946 when sixty-three female police officers were appointed to the Metropolitan (Tokyo) Police Department. As in West Germany, the shortage of manpower after the war changed the role of women quite dramatically.

By 1947, the use of policewomen had been so well received and so effective that the Ministry of Home Affairs stipulated to all national prefectual authorities that policewomen were to be integrated throughout Japan so that by 1953, 1,200 policewomen comprised over 3 percent of the total police establishment. The policewomen received the same salary, training and rank as male officers. In 1954, all the police agencies were reorganized and integrated into the National Police Agency, and the expansion of the policewoman's role continued.

Today, the policewomen in Japan have the same status and authority as male police officers, including police credentials and firearms. They are trained along with male recruits in an extensive six-month course at a police academy. The promotion to senior rank is open to those female officers who successfully pass the same promotional examination as male officers. Her duties include general police patrol, crime prevention, detective work, juvenile work and nearly the whole spectrum of law enforcement activities. She is even being used very innovatively to teach special traffic safety education courses for kindergarten children throughout Japan's schools. Presently policewomen total 1,500 throughout Japan. The Metropolitan Police (Tokyo) use 800 of their 1,100 policewomen on traffic control functions.[16]

Guyana

An interesting country to look at and to examine the usage of women in law enforcement is Guyana. This republic, created in 1970, has a population of approximately 760,000. One probably would not think that a small, new nation located on the northeast coast of South America would be using policewomen to any great extent, but they are.

From a small initial and experimental group of twelve women officers in 1953, the use of policewomen has expanded to comprise 7.5 percent of the total force. The female officers enjoy the same training, benefits, promotional opportunities and have the same powers as male officers. The public's reaction to policewomen has been very good, and today female officers are used in all positions that male officers occupy. Policewomen function as uniformed general patrol officers in vehicles and on foot. They perform specific patrol duties such as dealing with juveniles and dog patrol. They are used on the detective force and perform the whole range of police tasks.[17]

Sweden

Since the beginning of the twentieth century, women have, to a certain extent, been used in the Swedish police force. But until the mid-1950's, female personnel performed investigatory functions only. Female officers intended for executive police duties were employed for the first time in 1957. Having collected information from all the police commissioners in Sweden, the National Swedish Police Board decided, in consultation with the Swedish Policemen's Union, that female officers from the spring of 1970 onwards would be used mainly for criminal intelligence, criminal investigation and crime preventive duties and that they would not have to wear a uniform.

Since 1971, however, female officers perform the same duties as male officers and wear uniforms or plain clothes as their assignment demands. There are approximately 300 female officers out of a total 15,000 police officers or 2 percent of the force. Many of the females work in the greater metropolitan Stockholm area. The female officers have full police powers, receive the same training, promotional opportunities and benefits as male officers. Now as Swedish policewomen are starting to get into executive police positions the future looks good for the increase of female officers in Sweden.[18]

Norway

The employment of women in law enforcement in Norway is small and limited. Women have been associated with the Norway police for almost forty years, but it has only been in the last ten to fifteen years that policewomen worked in uniform. Policewomen have been and still are used in the traditional female police tasks, such as searching female prisoners, clerical duties and juvenile matters. But only 100 policewomen exist out of a total force of 5,500 officers, and most of these are employed in the metropolitan Oslo region.

The policewomen have the same powers, training and benefits as male officers. Their promotional opportunities are limited, though, and they are not utilized for police tasks where "their sex sets natural limitations when it is necessary to use force."[19]

Israel

Policewomen have functioned in Israel since 1960. Women perform a variety of police tasks, as well as providing security patrols for airports, hospitals, markets and schools. In 1969, 500 women from the army were assigned to the police to form a special unit to patrol the main roads and borders of Israel. Women officers comprise ninety percent of the excellent traffic police force. These traffic police not only give tickets to parking violators but also direct traffic and issue citations for moving violations.[20]

New Zealand

Women have been used on the New Zealand police force since 1942. Females entering the force have to meet different recruiting standards than men. Male recruits have to be between the ages of 19 and 35 years and at least 5'8½" tall, whereas females must be between the ages of 20 and 33 years with a height of not less than 5'5". Otherwise, male and female police recruits have to meet the same selection standards, and both undergo the same three-month course of training at the police academy.

The separate Women's Division, where policewomen were used to work primarily with women and children, was disbanded in 1966. Since women were granted equal pay with their male counterparts, the Commissioner of Police directed that women were to perform the same duties as men. In a study conducted in 1973 concerning the policewoman's role, it was found that she did not have equal job opportunities and equality of status with a male officer. As a result of this research, it has been decided that women will do exactly the same work as men in every facet of police work except that they will not be assigned to field duties on their own between the hours of 11 P.M. and 7 A.M. This recent policy is now receiving widespread acceptance and implementation.

Policewomen comprise about 2.4 percent of the total force of 3,214 officers. The females consist of three sergeants and seventy-four constables stationed throughout New Zealand. They have the same authority, receive the same benefits and have the same promotional opportunities as male officers.[21]

Conclusion

It is quite obvious that no clear-cut consensus exists in the countries of the world on the question of women in law enforcement. Aside from the countries discussed in this chapter, Denmark, Australia, Canada, Austria and other countries also use policewomen to one extent or another. There are, however, many countries today that do not use policewomen at all or use them very slightly. While some countries have enthusiastically adopted women on police agencies, others do not now nor have they ever considered using policewomen.

Even in the countries that employ policewomen, there is great variance in how they are utilized. Policewomen are almost nonexistent in France. They function on a very limited scope in Norway. Policewomen are utilized in all police functions in Great Britain and enjoy equal status, authority and benefits with male officers. So the situation in many, but not all, of the world's police agencies concerning policewomen is the same as it is in America: confused, hesitant and basically resistant toward new ideas and new ways of doing things.

REFERENCES

1. Chloe Owings, *Women Police* (Montclair, Patterson Smith Publishing Corporation, 1925), p. 25.
2. Owings, *Women Police*, p. 216.
3. Lois Higgins, "History of Women Police," *Proceedings of Workshop for Policewomen*, Nelson A. Watson and Robert N. Walker (Eds.) (Washington, International Association of Chiefs of Police, 1966), p. 31.
4. "The Metropolitan Women Police–A Historical Look," p. 2. (Mimeographed)
5. James Cramer, *World's Police* (London, Cassell and Company, Ltd., 1964), p. 35.
6. Based on personal correspondence between Deputy Assistant Commissioner, Personnel Department, of the Metropolitan Police Force, and the author on October 30, 1973.
7. *Ibid.*
8. British Information Services, *Women in Britain* (London, August 1971). R4497/71, p. 23.
9. Catherine Milton, *Women in Policing* (Washington, Police Foundation, 1972), p. 14.
10. George C. Berkeley, *The Democratic Policeman* (Boston, Beacon Press, 1969), pp. 68-69.

11. Milton, *Women in Policing*, pp. 13-14.
12. Stanislawa Paleolog, *The Women Police of Poland* (Westminster, The Association of Moral and Social Hygiene, 1945), pp. 21, 79.
13. Owings, *Women Police*, p. 70.
14. Berkeley, *The Democratic Policeman*, p. 69.
15. "La Police Moi J'Aime," *Paris-Match*, September 29, 1973, p. 79.
16. Associated Press dispatch, *The St. Louis Post-Dispatch*, September 15, 1973.
17. Based on personal correspondence between Commissioner of Police, Guyana, and the author on October 22, 1973.
18. Based on personal correspondence between Swedish National Police and the author on November 28, 1973.
19. Based on personal correspondence between Chief of Police, Trondheim, Norway, and the author on December 6, 1973.
20. Milton, *Women in Policing*, pp. 10, 14.
21. Based on personal correspondence between New Zealand Police National Headquarters and the author on December 28, 1973.

CHAPTER 3

THE HISTORY OF POLICEWOMEN IN AMERICA

WOMEN HAVE BEEN USED throughout American history as spies, undercover agents and detectives in agencies such as Pinkerton's, Wells Fargo and various United States intelligence organizations. But the need for sworn policewomen (with full police powers) has been recognized relatively recently.

The beginnings of this recognition came about during the first half of the nineteenth century. Women's organizations manifested an interest in the hiring of women for handling women and girls held in custody by publicly controlled institutions, such as the police and institutions for the insane.

In 1845, the first prison matrons were hired in New York City because of the efforts of the American Female Society. The use of prison matrons spread in the 1870's and 1880's. Then in 1888, Massachusetts and New York passed a law which made it mandatory for all cities with a population of over 20,000 to hire police matrons to care for female prisoners. These appointments of police matrons proved significant because they constitute the first mark of official recognition of the idea that women prisoners should be handled by women.[1]

In 1893, an appointment was made by the mayor of Chicago to provide for the widow of an officer. The police payroll carried Mrs. Marie Owens as a "patrolman" for thirty years until her retirement on pension. She visited courts and assisted detectives in cases involving women and children.

At the turn of the century, the movement for policewomen was strongly promulgated by such national groups as the Federation of Women's Clubs, the National League of Woman Voters, the National Women's Christian Temperance Union, local clubs and social agencies. In 1905 in Portland, Oregon, during the Lewis and Clark Expedition (a state exposition), a woman was given police powers to deal more effectively with problems involving girls and young women at the expedition. Mrs. Lola Baldwin was selected for this work because of her previous work as secretary with the National Traveler's Aid Association. Her work and its results proved so effective that Portland immediately organized a Department of Public Safety for the Protection of Young Girls and Women. Mrs. Baldwin became the first director of this division, later incorporated into the police department by charter. The women in it, though, remained known as "workers" or "operatives" rather than police.[2]

In 1910, the Los Angeles Police Department appointed the first regularly rated policewoman, Mrs. Alice Stebbins Wells, a graduate theological student and social worker. Mrs. Wells felt that social workers engaged in preventive and protective work for women and children would achieve better social results if they exercised police powers. She addressed a petition, containing the signatures of 100 influential citizens and civic organizations, to the police commission and the city council asking for an ordinance creating the position of policewoman.[3] After her appointment, Mrs. Wells' chief duties comprised the supervision and enforcement of laws concerning juveniles and women at dance halls, skating rinks, movie theaters and other similar places of public recreation. The appointment of Mrs. Wells as a policewoman attracted nationwide newspaper comment because she was an educated woman, a social worker and had deliberately sought and secured the opportunity to work in a police department. Many journalists presented a caricature of a policewoman as a bony, muscular, masculine person grasping a revolver. But many civic groups and police forces could see beyond the stereotype of the policewoman, and they deluged Mrs. Wells with questions and requests for her help in introducing policewomen into police agencies in their communities. Mrs. Wells became a pioneer in the national movement for policewomen's services as she lectured on policewomen around America and in many countries in the world.

By 1916, with Mrs. Wells' help, policewomen existed in twenty-five cities in twenty states and also in some foreign countries. Several women held executive positions in police agencies, too. The mayor of Milford, Ohio, even appointed Mrs. Dolly Spencer as a woman chief of police in 1914. She stayed on for two years to fight a gambling problem, only to be replaced when a new mayor took office.

An important event in the history of the policewomen's movement took place on May 17, 1915, when the International Association of Policewomen was organized. One of the initiators of the organization, Alice Stebbins Wells, became its first president.[4] The International Association of Chiefs of Police gave the policewomen support and assistance in formulating their own organization. The International Association of Policewomen contributed greatly to the well being of women police because of its constant search for better standards and its concern for the improvement of the role of policewomen. The association provided police agencies and the general public with information on policewomen. The International Association of Policewomen was unable to continue functioning, though, after its largest financial sponsor died in 1932, leaving the association hard pressed for funds during the peak of the depression.[5]

Women functioned in a quasi-police capacity during World War I around the military training camps in the country. They were employed by the Law Enforcement Division of the Commission on Training Camp Activities, which was charged with keeping prostitutes away from the camps, returning runaway women and girls to their homes and supervising commercial amusements near the camps. The outstanding work done by many women around the camps convinced some cities to try women on their police departments to work with women and children offenders. After the war, policewomen were employed in over 220 American cities.

At its convention in 1922, the International Association of Chiefs of Police passed a resolution that policewomen were essential to a modern police department. This aided the policewomen's movement in spreading into even more cities in the 1920's, which proved to be a decade of expansion for women in law enforcement. The success of women officers around the training camps and the active promotion of women police by the International Association of Policewomen caused this to come about. Also, people finally recognized that crime prevention, and not just repression and deterrence, was a legitimate function of the police.[6] Concurrently, people recognized that women performed as well as social workers and are effective in preventive work with other women and children. Yet policewomen of this time usually ended up in a separate Women's Bureau within a police department. Their duties, mostly preventive in nature, dealt with such areas as juvenile delinquency, female criminality, missing adults and juveniles and handling victims of sex offenses. Policewomen usually received less pay than male officers, also.

Of course, it was not smooth sailing for policewomen by any means. The average policeman and police chief thought of policewomen as a fad and considered their entry into the police field an unjustified excursion into social work.[7] They thought of punitive functions and not preventive ones as the duty of the police. No real concerted opposition to policewomen arose in the United States (unlike in Great Britain), but rather the attitude prevailed that women had to prove themselves good police officers which they most likely could not do.[8]

After 1930, there is an almost total lack of historical information on women in law enforcement. The Depression and its effects brought the hiring of female officers almost to a standstill. Although Massachusetts became the first state to employ female state police officers in 1930 and Connecticut did the same thing in 1943, only recently were women used on other state police agencies. During World War II, women reentered law enforcement to some degree to supplement manpower needs of police forces. They usually functioned as women auxiliary police, but after the war their use was terminated.

RECENT YEARS

There has been more discussion and experimentation with policewomen and greater use has been made of them in the last five years than at any other time in their history. Police administrators are seriously reevaluating their department's usage or nonusage of female officers. Various law enforcement agencies have experienced substantial changes which eventually will affect the entire American police community. These changes concerning the role of policewomen are taking place not just in one particular area of the country or on one size department. These changes occur now at all levels of government and in the private sector of law enforcement as well.

Federal Agencies

In July 1972, the first two women graduated the fourteen-week Federal Bureau of Investigation training course and were sworn in as agents. Presently, better than thirty female Special Agents exist out of a force of 8,500. The female agents must meet the same rigorous selection requirements as men. They also have the same authority, benefits, training and receive the same assignments as men. They will not be exempted from dangerous duties. In the past when the FBI needed a female for various assignments, they had to use an untrained female civilian clerk or "borrow" a policewoman from a local police force.

Of the 1,200 Special Agents of the Secret Service, seven of them are women. In the 109-year history of the Secret Service, only since December 1971, has it had female agents. As in the FBI, total equality between females and males exists in such areas as selection standards, authority, benefits, training and job assignments. The Executive Protective Service, the uniformed division of the Secret Service, guards the White House, the President's family, executive office buildings and foreign diplomatic missions in the Washington, D. C., metropolitan area. In 1970 this agency started employing women. Training, selection standards, benefits and authority are the same for men and women.[9]

Women now work in law enforcement capacities on other Federal agencies such as the Drug Enforcement Administration and the U. S. Customs Service also. The Military Police of the Army now use female MP's. In the spring of 1973, twenty Women's Army Corps volunteers were selected for the first women's military police training program at Fort Gordon, Georgia. They have since graduated and been assigned to MP units around the country. The U. S. Marine Corps has recently started to train females for military police duty also. Although women employed by Federal agencies enjoy equal status with men, it is unclear whether or not various agencies employ a quota system on the number or percentage of females being hired by any one agency.

State Police

Although women have been employed by Massachusetts and Connecticut state police forces for a number of years, their role has been limited. In Connecticut, fourteen women are members of the state police, but none of them are uniformed troopers. They wear civilian clothes, do not perform general patrol duties and are usually assigned to juvenile and sex crime cases.[10] This role appears to be changing, though, as nearly two hundred women recently participated in a state troopers' entrance examination. Until last spring Connecticut law limited the number of female state police officers, but now this barrier has been removed.

The Pennsylvania State Police became the first state police agency to employ women for state police duties identical to those performed by men. This occurred in July 1972, as the first fourteen female troopers to graduate from the training academy went to stations throughout the state for general patrol duties and other assignments, as the need arose. Since then thirteen more women troopers entered the force.[11]

Female state police officers now work in Michigan and New York, too. Just recently, the Texas Department of Public Safety, the Maine State Police, Illinois State Police, and the California Highway Patrol announced they would consider female applicants for general patrol positions. So change with respect to women's role in law enforcement is occurring on the state level as well.

Private Security Agencies

Private security agencies are big business in the United States. Almost 300,000 people work for private security services and equipment companies. The scope of activities that private security agencies are involved in is great. They provide such services as college campus security, guards for all types of companies and institutions, private investigation and many, many others. Although most employees of private companies do not have full police powers of arrest, they are often armed and perform many quasi-law enforcement functions. Pinkerton, the nation's oldest and largest private security company, employs 36,000 people, with 4,000 female guards and detectives. Female private security officers work to some extent on college campuses, airport security details, retail store security, plant protection and many other areas. Females perform not only as line personnel but also as supervisors and managers. Still, though, the use of women in private security agencies remains limited. In the entire area of private security throughout the country, women comprise only 5.4 percent of the personnel employed in 1960.[12]

Local Police Forces

The local city and county police agencies employ the largest number of personnel in the public area of law enforcement. Therefore, the actions of local level police departments determine if a change in the usage of policewomen will take place in America. In recent years, a number of police forces have experimented with and, in some cases, adopted changes in the woman's role.

Indianapolis emerged as the first American city to assign policewomen to general patrol duty. In September 1968, two female officers began to patrol the streets in Car 47. Although the experiment lacked sound planning, and the policewomen received only on-the-job training, today the women have been grudgingly accepted, as they have proved that they can handle the job. Initially, male officers and radio dispatchers felt reluctant to have them handle any field situations but by February 1972, eight patrolwomen were assigned to Car 47. This allows a two-person patrol unit to operate seven days a week on the day and evening shifts. They handle calls in high crime areas and calls for assistance just as male officers do. The public seems to accept them, and female complainants often express relief that female, instead of male, officers talk with them.[13]

The Indianapolis usage of policewomen is paradoxical, though. Policewomen comprise 7.3 percent of the total force of 1,149; however, only fourteen of the 74 policewomen do any field police work. Well over one-half the policewomen, including most of the sergeants, work in a secretarial or clerical capacity. Fourteen women serve as radio dispatchers. Five women work as plainclothes narcotic investigators, and twelve of the department's 42 juvenile officers are females.[14]

The Peoria, Illinois Police Department falls in the medium-sized department range with 209 policemen and nine policewomen. Seven of the nine women perform general patrol duties; the other two work in the juvenile bureau. Under Chief Allen H. Andrews, Peoria has made some significant gains in the use of policewomen.

All of Peoria's policewomen on general patrol duty have trained for and handled all types of calls in the city's high-crime area. Initially, the tendency of some policemen and civilian dispatchers to be over-protective of the patrolwomen constituted the main problem. This situation has improved considerably as the policewomen have proved that they can handle the dangerous and potentially dangerous situation. Chief Andrew's feelings are that since policewomen get equal pay with males, they should perform equal work. This they have done.[15]

As of today though, policewomen are recruited under a quota system and only nine "slots" are allocated for them on the department. Also, separate civil service and promotional lists are maintained for men and women. The on-going evaluation of the performance of policewomen continues in Peoria; if the experiment proves positive, an increased role for females should emerge.[16]

The Miami, Florida Police Department has been using policewomen innovatively in recent years. In 1965, they equalized the educational requirements for females with males. Previously, women had to have a college degree whereas males only had to have a high school diploma. Today, though, Chief Bernard Garmire believes that policewomen should be given the same responsibilities as policemen.

Miami has 29 policewomen on a force of 755. Of these 29, all except two are assigned to field operations divisions. Four policewomen in the patrol division perform general patrol duties in solo and two-officer patrol vehicles which supplement regular one-officer patrol units in high crime areas. One of these female officers serves as a sector sergeant who supervises eight patrolmen. Six policewomen are assigned to the traffic division where they perform as accident investigators and "traffic controllers" at specific intersections. They usually operate alone. Nine female officers assigned to criminal investigations and special investigations work with and without partners as the situation demands. One of the females even investigates homicides.

The policewomen have been well received by the public for they have performed well in many potentially dangerous situations. Chief Garmire foresees an expanded role for policewomen with his department as they prove themselves and become assimilated into the police force.[17]

The New York City Police Department is the largest in the nation with 31,000 officers. Of this total, 735, or more than 2 percent, are female officers. The number increased sharply after the results of the December 15, 1973, Civil Service test for police applicants were announced. New York had its first single exam for the position of police officer. Previously, separate tests and hiring and promotion quotas in the department existed for females. About 16,000 females of the 53,474 people took the exam. Since New York City has dropped its height and weight selection standards (weight in proportion to height, though), female and male applicants have to meet the same selection standards. Aside from the same exam given to applicants of both sexes, there will be an identical physical fitness exam, too. It will consist of an agility test, a simulated body carry, sit-ups and a one-mile run in under twelve minutes.

Women have not always enjoyed this equality with men on the New York Police force. Only in 1965 was the first policewoman allowed (after a court order) to take the sergeant's exam and was then appointed to that position. In 1968, after the separate Women's Bureau was disbanded, the department's policewomen were then assigned to various duties around the city. Policewomen worked traditionally as jail matrons, handled juvenile cases and performed clerical tasks. Today, New York City experiences a vast change in the use of its policewomen. Approximately 400 female officers are assigned to car and foot patrols performing general patrol duties. This developed after a one-year experiment (started in May 1972) with fourteen women officers in three different precincts which proved that females could perform field patrol functions satisfactorily. Most of the females are on the street with male partners and have handled themselves well.

Policewomen in New York perform virtually every police task including plainclothes detective, juvenile and community-relations work. Women have not moved up the promotional ladder in any significant numbers, though. Only two female officers hold the rank of captain or higher. One of these women, Captain Vittoria Renzullo, is the second in command of a 175-officer police precinct in Manhattan. An interesting and successful utilization of policewomen occurred in January 1973. The police department initiated a Rape Analysis and Investigation Section, an all female unit designed to help combat the city's rising rape statistics. This unit was headed by Lieutenant Julia Tucker who stated that "women find it easier to talk to women detectives . . . they remember certain details which establishes a certain pattern for us."[18] Having female officers interview female victims of sex offenses has developed leads about the offenders which male officers have failed to get in interviews. St. Louis and several other police departments are in the process of creating female or male-female officer rape squads.

All is not "smooth sailing" for policewomen in New York City, though. Many male officers still lack the conviction that females can handle general patrol duties. Further, the wives of some officers are quite upset with the use of women in field patrol. Some of the wives appear motivated by jealousy and others by fear for their husband's safety. But change in the role of policewomen on the New York department is here to stay.[19]

The Metropolitan Police Department of Washington, D. C. is one of the most innovative departments in the country in its usage of policewomen. Of course, this was not always the case. In 1967, they disbanded the separate women's bureau. Since 1918, when the bureau was established, all policewomen assigned to it were considered specialists in the juvenile and female crime area. Their hiring standards, different from men's, stated that women had to have a college degree and be at least five feet one inch. Men had to have only a high school diploma and be at least five feet seven inches tall.

In July 1969, a program began under the new Chief of Police, Jerry Wilson, to promote a greater utilization of policewomen and evaluation of their performance in various new functions not traditionally assigned to women. The selection requirements for women applicants changed to match those for men except weight. They allotted 110 positions to women. Until uniforms were designed and ordered for policewomen, they worked as investigators, vice officers, juvenile officers, clerks and in almost every area outside of uniformed patrol. After the uniforms arrived in December 1971, Chief Wilson announced that women would be assigned the entire range of police duties including general patrol. On January 21, 1972, the Department started to recruit 100 more women officers to perform patrol duty on an experimental basis. (Currently, 300 women are employed throughout this department of 5,100 officers.)

In this important experiment, 107 policewomen, assigned to two

districts, performed all phases of patrol work. They worked interchangeably with male officers and were evaluated by the same criteria as males. Preliminary findings of this experiment, based on an
average of four months patrol duty for each woman officer, have
been released in *Policewoman on Patrol*, a three part study published by the Urban Institute and Police Foundation. These preliminary findings show that policewomen do as well as policemen on
patrol duty. It will be at least until May 1974, though, before all the
evidence is in and a continuation study is published. Then after six-
teen months as a field patrol officer, the policewomen's performance
can be truly evaluated.[20]

St. Louis County Police Department has employed policewomen
in some capacity since the department's inception in 1965. In 1972
the role of the county's female officers was broadened to include
the general patrol function. Under a year long experiment run by
Dr. Lewis Sherman of the University of Missouri at St. Louis,
women were recruited into the department for eventual deployment
in one-person patrol units. The women were given the same training as male recruits in a four-month training academy. Their performance has been evaluated and will be discussed more in Chapter
6. Presently, four percent of the county's 550 officers are females.
Most of these twenty-two policewomen are in the patrol division.
The county department has just recently dropped the minimum
height and weight standards for police officers, thereby facilitating
the recruitment of more females. The department's head administrator, Superintendent Kleinknecht, supports the program and predicts
a greater role for policewomen in the future on the county's force.[21]

SUMMARY

Aside from the local police departments discussed, other American cities have been utilizing policewomen in innovative ways in
recent years. Morro Beach, California, assigned three policewomen
to field patrol duties. Philadelphia uses several women in its Civil
Disobedience Unit for duty at demonstrations, strikes and riots. The
Los Angeles County Sheriffs Department has the highest percentage
of policewomen on its department of any medium- or large-sized
police department in the country. Slightly more than 8 percent, or
390 members, of the force are policewomen. They have been em-

ployed in every aspect of police work except general patrol for years. Presently, though, female officers even serve on an experimental basis in general patrol.

Still, with the positive changes seen on several departments concerning their use of policewomen, it would be a mistake for the reader to assume that policewomen are used in nontraditional assignments and to any significant extent on a nationwide law enforcement basis. On local police agencies throughout the country approximately 6,000 policewomen comprise slightly less than two percent of the sworn police officer population.[22] Almost all of these women are employed in urban areas and are used on less than forty percent of the departments in the country.[23] This small percentage of women officers can also be seen on the state and federal level and in private security as well. Although women perform patrol duties in several communities, the number of policewomen doing this is probably no more than 900 nationwide. Truly, women still fulfill their traditional tasks on most police agencies, i.e. juvenile officers, clerical personnel, sex crime investigators and handling female prisoners.

REFERENCES

1. Lois Higgins, "History of Women Police," *Proceedings of Workshop for Policewomen.* Nelson A. Watson and Robert N. Walker (Eds.) (Washington, International Association of Chiefs of Police, 1966), p. 21.
2. Chloe Owings, *Women Police* (Montclair, Patterson Smith Publishing Corporation, 1925), p. 100.
3. Alice Stebbins Wells, "Reminiscences of a Policewoman," *The Police Reporter*, September 1929, p. 23.
4. Wells, "Reminiscences of a Policewoman," p. 24.
5. Higgins, "History of Women Police," pp. 31-32.
6. Lois Higgins, *Policewoman's Manual* (Springfield, Charles C Thomas, 1961), p. XIV.
7. Eleanore L. Hutzel, *The Policewoman's Handbook* (Worcester, Columbia University Press, 1933), p. 3.
8. Owings, *Women Police*, p. 203.
9. Letty Cottin Pogrebin, "The Working Woman," *Ladies' Home Journal*, September 1973, pp. 36, 38.
10. *New York Times*, August 4, 1973, Section II, pp. 1, 50, cols. 1-2.
11. Gloria Stevenson, "The Force of Change," *Occupational Outlook Quarterly*, Winter, 1972, pp. 11-15.
12. James Kakalik and Sorrel Wildhorn, *The Private Police Industry: Its*

Nature and Extent, U. S. Department of Justice, Vol. II, No. R-870/DOJ (Washington, Government Printing Office), p. 139.

13. Catherine Milton, *Women in Policing* (Washington, Police Foundation, 1972), pp. 62-66.
14. Based on personal correspondence between Indianapolis Police Department and the author on January 10, 1974.
15. Milton, *Women in Policing*, pp. 76-82.
16. Based on personal correspondence between Peoria Police Department and the author on January 14, 1974.
17. Based on personal correspondence between Miami Police Department and the author on January 21, 1974.
18. *New York Post*, January 10, 1973, pp. 3, 29, cols. 1-2.
19. *New York Times*, November 10, 1973, Section I, pp. 1, 29, cols. 1, 3.
20. P. Bloch, D. Anderson, and P. Gervais, *Policewomen on Patrol*, Vol. 1 (Washington, Police Foundation, February 1973), pp. 50-64.
21. Statement by Dr. Lewis Sherman during personal interview, February 13, 1974.
22. U. S. National Advisory Commission on Criminal Justice Standards and Goals, *Report on Police* (Washington, Government Printing Office, 1973), p. 343.
23. Milton, *Women in Policing*, p. 16.

CHAPTER 4

OBSTACLES CONFRONTING WOMEN IN LAW ENFORCEMENT

FIRST, a clarification of the term "policewoman" is necessary. Perhaps this clarification is overdue at this stage of the book, but a very incisive definition of a policewoman was formulated at the International Association of Chiefs of Police workshop on policewomen held in 1966:

> A policewoman is a sworn peace officer, empowered to enforce all of the laws and ordinances of the jurisdiction and to detect and arrest violators, and ~~is appointed for the increased moral protection of~~ women and minors and for the ~~prevention of delinquency among such women and minors, and for such other police duties as can best be perfor~~med ~~by a woman~~.
> Like the policeman, the policewoman is subject to the rules, regulations, and disciplinary procedures of the department and is entitled to the same rights, salary, privileges, and opportunities.[1]

This definition then does not include a woman who is a "meter maid," a school crossing guard, a jail matron (a woman correctional officer with limited or no police power who handles female prisoners) or a secretary employed by a police agency. The policewoman is not part of the growing trend of employing civilian women to perform an increasing variety of peripheral or nonenforcement duties. Rather, the policewoman is a sworn female member of a police department with full police powers.

To what extent, then, do departments use women in police work today? In 1966, the International Association of Chiefs of Police (IACP) conducted a survey in 161 police departments of the largest cities in forty-seven states. The cities surveyed have a total population of some 70 million or a little less than one third of the people of America. Yet, these departments employ only 1,792 female police officers with full police powers. Many sizable cities have no policewomen at all. In the cities where women officers work, no discernible pattern of use of women nor any consistency in the ratio of female to male officers existed. The percentage of policewomen to male officers in ten of the larger cities in the United States ranged from a high of 2.25 to a low of .05 of 1 percent of the force. Also of interest, this survey found that most policewomen serve under male officers and that few women had command positions at any level.[2]

In a recent comprehensive survey of police personnel practices, the IACP and the nonprofit Police Foundation found that women constitute less than 2 percent of the nation's sworn police officers. The agencies responding to a questionnaire represented a total of 166,000 police officers; policewomen totaled only 2,859. This report also noted that very few women hold command positions in police departments.[3]

Historically and traditionally, law enforcement has been viewed as a crime suppressive task performed by men. After an individual broke the law, the police went out, arrested him and brought him to trial. This emerged as the clear-cut role for law enforcement officers in the criminal justice system of America and the world to perform. Not until the nineteenth century was the practical value of prevention and reform recognized. As already pointed out in previous chapters, the use of policewomen developed concurrently with this change in law enforcement philosophy.

Even today, though, many law enforcement officers still view the police role as suppressive in nature and, therefore, a man's job. Various male and female attitudes in the general population and in police circles aided in the creation of some very formidable obstacles that women seeking or pursuing a career in policing must face. These attitudes in and of themselves present a major obstacle to be discussed later in this chapter. The other obstacles stem to an extent from individual and societal values and attitudes, but they seem to stand alone, as well. These obstacles (both obvious and subtle ones) have served to limit the numbers and effectiveness of policewomen.

One prominent obstacle, which will not be discussed here, is the question of a female's physical capability (or lack of it) to perform general police patrol duties. This will be dealt with in depth in Chapter 6 while looking at the question of policewomen in general patrol. Even without this factor, the following obstacles have also helped keep policewomen out of many different aspects of police work (other than general patrol) and out of many different police departments.

The Selection Process

The selection process constitutes one of the crucial areas that has to be examined to determine if a police agency is or will be successful in its role performance. The way an agency selects its recruits has a far-reaching and long-lasting effect. If a poor or meaningless selection process exists, then poor caliber officers will be recruited who will eventually perform poorly in the field. For a police department to be successful in dealing with crime and community aid, it must select its recruits carefully. Police recruits should be chosen on the basis of whether or not they will effectively carry out the police officer's job. But two ideas are implicit in that statement. First, what *truly* is a police officer's job? What does he really do on an average shift? Secondly, how does a police department test and select an officer to perform the real police role?

Many law enforcement agencies select their recruits by administering written, general aptitude exams having no relationship to anything in police work. Then the agencies apply other meaningless, nonjob-related standards to the prospective employee in order to separate the "wheat from the chaff." But existing selection requirements and procedures in the majority of police departments do not screen out unfit candidates.

Of course, this poor selection process presents the first of several obstacles that a woman entering the field of law enforcement encounters. The odds against a female recruit's selection are high because the selection process and standards have been stacked against her. Furthermore, many departments have special entrance requirements for males and females. Women job applicants usually have to meet higher educational requirements, smaller height and weight standards and take entrance examinations that differ in emphasis from the men's. In fact, in a recent study of national police selection standards, a number of police departments require higher educational levels for women than for men. In some departments women could not receive consideration for employment without a college degree, whereas men needed only a high school diploma or an equivalency certificate.[4] The rationale offered for higher female education levels and different entrance exams (written and oral) is that policewomen work mostly in the juvenile area. The educational level and the exams emphasize this youth and "social problems" role of policewomen.

Minimum height requirements averaged out nationally at 5'8" for men and 5'5" for women (weight in proportion to height). But some departments maintain the woman's height standard at the same high level as the male's.[5] This then discriminates against the majority of women not usually that tall. Some police agencies also have different minimum and maximum entrance ages for men and women, with the females again being discriminated against.

The key factor for the nation's police forces is that most of the selection standards and procedures are not job-related and are, therefore, not valid. They have not proved significant in determining job performance one way or another. Who says a police officer has to be 5'8" to be effective? And if we say females can be effective at 5'5", why not males at that height, also? Departments need selection standards and procedures. But they have to be valid standards in relationship to the job the person is hired for, and if college proves necessary for a female juvenile officer, why not for the male patrol officer who deals with the whole community. All of the selection standards of a department need to be examined and reevaluated. Should they be considered valid standards or primarily meaningless discriminatory ones? Law enforcement can ill afford to turn away good career candidates on the basis of poor standards. So departments should raise or lower standards where necessary after experimentation and then apply them equally to members of both sexes. If a required level of strength and agility proves necessary for police officers, then a valid test should be drawn up to determine this. Females and males should take the same physical agility test. Then it would not matter whether a recruit is 5'8" or 5'4", or a male or female, but only whether he/she possesses the physical capability to do the job. The New York City Police Department has recently dropped their minimum height and weight requirements because they felt these were not job-related. They created a valid physical strength and agility test, though, which prospective officers of both sexes take.

Of course, all this talk concerning fair and valid selection standards will remain pointless for females trying to get on police departments with official or "unofficial" female quotas. Very few police administrators will say "outfront" that they have a quota for policewomen in their department. The various laws prohibiting official quotas and their effectiveness will be discussed in detail later in the book. But obviously "unofficial" quotas have existed and still exist (laws notwithstanding) on many police agencies. Just too many police departments have "had only three policewomen for ten years" or have "just hired the first policewoman since 1956" and so on. We see the quota system quite clearly in cities which maintain separate male and female civil service eligibility lists. The fact that women's examination scores may be higher than those of men is not considered until the police department decides to hire more women. The Police Foundation found out that every department that they had surveyed stops hiring women long before they meet their total police personnel needs.[6] Thus, qualified and talented people are kept out of law enforcement for no other reason than their sex. Police agencies should not turn away good candidates because they cannot meet their personnel needs with present policies. Almost 70 percent of the police departments around the country work below authorized strength with the average large city force being 10 percent below.[7] Official and unofficial quotas must be eliminated so that qualified and skilled police recruits of both sexes can help meet personnel needs. Separate male and female eligibility lists should be combined where candidates seek the same job.

Training

Once a police recruit has been selected, training becomes the next important step to consider. Without proper training, the recruit will not develop into a fully qualified and effective police officer. The training has to be relevant and thorough. A recruit without adequate training remains limited in usefulness to his department.

In many communities policewomen have been given separate training from male recruits. Since they were only going to be used in a juvenile or secretarial capacity, why waste time and money on firearms training or self-defense classes? This separate and inadequate training of female police recruits has further limited their role in police agencies. Occasionally, when policewomen have been assigned to jobs for which they have not been trained (usually field assignments), the females have either performed poorly, or male partners have felt it necessary to protect them to the detriment of the assignment.[8]

As women police officers are recruited and utilized by police agencies, then they too must receive comprehensive training. The top police administrator must see that all police recruits have adequate training.

In order to insure integration and cohesion between male and female officers, both sexes should be trained together at a police academy. Men and women should be in the same training classes, learning the same subjects and doing the same physical and firearms exercises. The author has gone through a police academy in a class of both men and women and has clearly seen how being trained together fosters teamwork and respect for the other person's ability, male or female. This respect carries over into the field after training. Women develop pride in themselves and their capabilities as they realize they can "hold their own" with male officers in physical training, on the firing range and in the academic field. Male officers, seeing that policewomen can perform and function under the stress of training, change some of their skeptical attitudes toward women to those of respect and camaraderie. The benefits derived from male and female officers training together are immeasurable. This factor of a shared group experience in a training situation may be a key to the reduction of sexist attitudes in male officers. Thus it is imperative that male and female officers train together on every police department.

Benefits

Historically, many police departments have not paid policewomen the same salary as policemen. Nor have women enjoyed the same promotional opportunities. True, in some cases the female officers were only used as a "glorified" clerk-typist and not deserving of the same salary as a male officer. But in many such instances female officers received less pay than male officers who performed the same type of work. Even today salary discrimination still works against female officers on various departments.

Recently, the author spoke to a policewoman who had just received an out-of-court settlement from her city government. She had been a juvenile officer. Males in that job automatically received a detective's salary, two steps more than the police officer's salary. This policewoman had not been paid at the higher salary. With the help of a city councilwoman, she forced the city to "see the light" and meet her legitimate demand of equal pay for equal work. But many male officers have questioned whether policewomen should get the same salary as men when women are not used in field situations where danger exists. The author has heard this comment from policemen several times, so it is not a superfluous question. The following statements typify the feeling held by most policewomen concerning the issue of equal pay:

> My life is imperiled just as well as theirs (male officers). I may not be out as often as they are: but, still, from my going to court from time to time, there are still nuts which could be pursuing me, which I brought to court. I've gotten threatening phone calls, also. Maybe I don't meet the same number of resisting type of criminals as a male field officer, but my life is still imperiled as well as theirs. And I am still, by standing up there and taking that oath, I have marked myself as a separate entity in the population. I could be in a store and some dude that I've handled before say, for instance, "Hey, man, there's a pig, we're going to get her." Regardless of whether she's female or male, she represents the "man" and I could be "offed" (as they say) just as well as anyone else (9).

> I could be shot at any time. I drive a radio car around. I go into and out of stations. I had one occasion where a Mafia member was in the station and saw me. Now he knows me and my car, and my license number. You know he knows me. Now my life is in jeopardy. If they would ever feel that a blonde cop turned them in or saw them do something, they might go after me. You still run the risks of being in a station where there is going to be a bombing, having an inmate attack you, and doing all these things . . . Now I can see how a homicide detective who sometimes has to work forty-eight hours straight would resent a gal who does office work just eight hours a day getting the same salary as he gets. But what he fails to realize, too, is the number of men doing "nonfield" tasks and getting the same pay also (12).

The last policewoman makes a very good point. Many male field (patrol or detective) officers do resent an officer with a nice "safe" desk job getting the same salary as they do. But one has to realize that many male officers in this category get equal pay for less hazardous work. Of course more women percentage-wise fall in this area of protected "inside" jobs, but whose fault is that? Male administrators have assigned women to a limited role in the police agencies. A policewoman comments:

> Whenever I've gotten into any discussion with a male officer concerning the equal pay "rap," I think that I've presented my views in such a way that they have to agree. I'm all for giving the patrol officer a hazard pay or whatever arrangements they can make so that he is compensated for the dangers that he encounters. But I think that our jobs (policewomen) are comparable to male officers right down the line outside of patrol, therefore we deserve the equal pay (28).

Perhaps this would provide an equitable solution. Give officers involved in hazard duty assignments a bonus pay; officers performing nonhazardous pay would not receive this bonus. This type of pay differential should not be given on the basis of an officer's sex but on an officer's job description and classification. Policewomen should get equal pay for equal work with policemen.

The promotional opportunities for policewomen are limited on most of the nation's police departments. The Police Foundation found in a recent study that very few policewomen hold supervisory positions.[9] Some departments do not permit policewomen to take or even apply for promotional exams. This practice would seem to be illegal, but so much for police agencies and their view of the law. Others allow women to take promotional exams and award promotions only in "women's positions." Since women have been utilized mostly in the juvenile, secretarial and female prisoner areas, then this, too, is where their limited promotional opportunities are. Policewomen in departments with this policy cannot take a promotional exam until one of the few supervisory "slots" becomes vacant. This often meant that the officer had to wait until the supervisor died or retired before she could even consider promotion.

Catherine Milton in an excellent book, *Women in Policing*, felt that "it is ironic that so many departments have high education requirements for women who want to enter policing and then they deny them promotional opportunities open to less educated men." Also, policewomen are assigned primarily specialized "inside" tasks, and then they are denied supervisory spots in these areas where talent and skill are the key job requisites.[10] Just like entrance requirements, promotional requirements must be based on an officer's ability to do a job. Meaningful and objective performance evaluation standards must be drawn up and applied equally to male and female officers. Separate promotional lists should be combined and equal promotional opportunities should be authorized for female police officers.

A police chief should be filling a supervisory position with his most skilled and qualified person, regardless of sex, color, height and all the other false criteria which do not determine who will be a good supervisor.

Former Deputy Commissioner Melchionne comments on female police supervisors.

> Recently, the extension of promotional opportunities to policewomen in some jurisdictions has added new dimensions to the administrator's evaluation of the status of women in his organization. The enlightened police administrator, of course, recognizes that sound personnel practice mandates the establishment of career development opportunities for all personnel—policewomen included. How else can morale, enthusiasm, and motivation for professional development be maintained?[11]

The police chief who does not provide equal promotional opportunities for his department's policewomen stifles their desire and pride, and possibly deprives the department and community of some very able and skilled police supervisors.

Generalist and Specialist

Traditionally, women have been considered specialists on law enforcement agencies. They received separate training in a police academy (in some cases not trained at all) and then are assigned to work as a secretary-clerk, jail matron or juvenile officer. Males entering police work have mostly been considered generalists. After the academy training, the male probationary officer was usually assigned to general field patrol. Departments felt (and still do today) that male officers should get a broad base of experience concerning police work and that the best place to do this was on the street.

Then, perhaps, after several years on patrol, the male officer could try to get one of the specialized jobs on the department. Specialized jobs have always been considered "prestige" positions by most police personnel. Officers perform many of these type jobs in civilian clothes and have fairly regular hours (9:00-5:00) with weekends off.

So then what is the problem? It appears that females have benefited by being considered specialists and getting assigned automatically to prestige jobs. There are several problems with this tradition of specialization, though. One of the most obvious problems has been male resentment towards female officers. Many males want the specialist jobs with the status and benefits, but they have had to work for several years in patrol before even being considered. So whereas the male advances to the specialized positions by merit or experience, the female is assigned to these positions on the basis of her gender. This generates much male animosity towards the women.

Another key problem with female specialization has been women's lack of vital field patrol experience. For the "field" is what a police department is all about. Many police administrators feel that an officer has to be a field generalist before he can be an effective specialist. By skipping over this exposure to the field, policewomen not only lack this necessary knowledge, but also they are then limited as to what jobs they can be assigned. In addition to limitation in jobs, the policewoman finds her promotional opportunities restricted as well. While the majority of supervisory positions exist in the patrol division, departments feel that field supervisors must have had field experience in order to be effective and respected by subordinates. The policewoman cannot be assigned these supervisory positions then without the field experience.

This tradition of special treatment and specialization has hindered rather than helped the policewoman in her law enforcement career. Another area of policewomen specialization (and separation from the rest of the department) exists in the organizational structure of some police departments. Traditionally, most large cities employing policewomen assigned them to separate women's divisions within the department.[12] Today, though, the trend deemphasizes separate women's divisions. Of course, the policewoman's placement in the organizational structure of a department depends to a large extent on the size of the department and the number of women employed.

Some people feel that in large urban departments (with a substantial number of policewomen),

> the police administrator may find it expedient to establish a central-ized women's division, headed by a woman and staffed by police-women superior officers selected under civil service. In addition to normal policewoman functions, such a woman's division can operate as a personnel pool for all units of the department having short-term, intermittent need of a policewoman's services. This arrangement does not prevent long-term deployment of policewomen to other appro-priate units of the department, where desirable.[13]

New York City Police Department, with the largest number of po-licewomen in America, employed this women's division concept for many years in their organizational structure. In other departments, with a small number of policewomen, all the women may be de-ployed to juvenile or an investigative unit or to the office of the po-lice chief.

The only valid reason for placing a policewoman in any part of the organization should be whether she can aid the police depart-ment by filling a certain position. All police officers should be as-signed where they can help the department the most. In some depart-ments, it may be necessary and prove effective to assign police-women to a woman's division or just to one unit such as juvenile. The individual needs and desires of a police department will de-termine the best place for policewomen in the organizational struc-ture.

The existence of a separate women's division or unit has some ad-vantages, though, that some female and male officers are reluctant to see changed. "To a policeman, it means he will not be in direct competition with women for advancement, that he will not be su-pervised by women and that he will not have to be involved with them in a protector-partner role."[14] Some policewomen feel that as a separate unit dealing with juveniles and females, they are more ef-fective than working with male officers who do not consider this "real" police work. A separate women's division also has some other significance to policewomen. They have opportunity for advance-ment within their own division, and upon promotion they enjoy full power and responsibility. Women who are supervised by women do not have to take orders from men nor engage in partnerships with overly protective male officers.

But because the creation of separate sections (whether in a woman's division or a juvenile bureau) for policewomen runs many risks, they do not benefit women or the department in the long run. For women's bureaus run the risk of isolation and a lack of cooperation with other sections of the department. A police chief should avoid creating independent women's police units because they may tend to drift from the main organization and perhaps become somewhat despised by their coworkers.[15] The primary goal of a police chief should be to infuse policewomen into all parts of his organization and at all levels. Male and female officers must be integrated and learn to work together as a team for maximum effectiveness. The policewomen must identify with the goals and aims of the entire police organization and not see themselves as auxiliary specialists.[16] Separate women's bureaus do not help to achieve cohesiveness in a police department.

Police agencies will still need some degree of specialization in the future. But specialists should be assigned on the basis of their talent and experience, not their sex. Policewomen should be treated as generalists until they prove themselves and earn a specialized position. Separate selection criteria, training, benefits, promotional opportunities and assignments have all helped to keep the policewoman in her "place." She has not been in a position of "separate but equal," but "separate and unequal." If crime is to be curtailed in this country, then an effective integration of all personnel and resources must challenge it.

Attitudes

The obstacles discussed so far in this chapter remain very real and concrete. These major obstacles or variations of them have impeded the progress of policewomen in America. Police administrators, aware of these obstacles, must deal with them if they are to fully utilize policewomen in their departments. But what caused these obstacles in the first place? What is the real motivation behind them?

With examination of these obstacles and with the facade removed, the true essence emerges. At the core of the whole issue of women in law enforcement is the word *attitudes*. Attitudes constitute the "nitty-gritty" of this issue. Attitudes of male officers towards policewomen have had the most effect on the obstacles. But female attitudes have also helped shape and modify the obstacles before police-

women, to some extent. And, of course, the community as a whole
has influenced the issue too. The difficulty in examining and discussing attitudes is that while they are very real, they are not tangible nor
something one can put a finger on and say, "correct this or change
that." Let us look at "attitudes" to see how they have formed and
shaped other obstacles.

Negative male attitudes towards women in law enforcement have
been the most significant factor in hindering the advancement of
policewomen. No solid proof supports this male bias against policewomen, but none is needed since males run the police departments.
The general feeling was, and still is, among the majority of male officers, that "police work is a man's work." Women are not emotion-
ally or physically equipped to handle this man's job of policing. Policewomen should only be used in certain areas away from the violence and sordidness of everyday police work.

The author asked the policewomen quoted in this section about
obstacles confronting a woman in the field of law enforcement. The
following statements give their perspective on *obstacles* and male
attitudes that have shaped them.

> Her being a female, period. Limited in regard to things you are going
> to be allowed to do in spheres and it is not just by prejudice that men
> have who are in the bureau or in the department themselves, it's the
> public opinion of what a woman should be doing . . . Sometimes it has
> happened that women could be advanced and maintain certain posi-
> tions but because of the public and because of built-in prejudice
> against women, period, they (the police) just can't promote women to
> a wide degree of supervisional jobs (9).

> Built-in resistance from the men themselves . . . You have the re-
> sistance of "old-line" command and when I say "old-line" command,
> I mean members of a given department that have been around a long
> time that have some very, perhaps, distasteful things happen to them
> when they've had ladies working for them. And that has spoiled it
> for everyone else and rather than being very objective, perhaps, and
> realizing that was just an isolated incident, maybe they just were guilty
> of tabloid thinking and this you'll have throughout the country . . . So
> you're trying to work yourself into a male orientated field and it's
> male orientated from the public's viewpoint and departmental per-
> sonnel (11).

> Discrimination quite a bit, probably, not *per se*, but there are some
> things that we (women) can't do and men can do and I think they re-

sent our being here . . . I've probably had to work much harder at my job than some of the guys in order to prove myself. I feel that the males are looking at me in a very critical light. I am a sergeant, also, and I know many of the guys think, "well, if she weren't here I probably could have a job," but I think this is only human nature and this would probably apply to anyone (6).

In viewing various attitudes and obstacles confronting policewomen, some things must be kept in mind. Policemen and policewomen are job categories that individual males and females fill. These people live in the whole context of male and female spheres in America today. These male and female roles have been shaped and modified by history, society and the individual. So traditional roles and stereotyped ways of acting and thinking have influenced both sexes. The next two policewomen express quite clearly the influence that traditional roles and stereotypes have had on policewomen:

> Policewomen are still predominantly used in the juvenile and matron areas where they have always been historically used. I think we're limited to these areas because it's the old adage of women with their place in the home . . . I think it's due to male resistance and also too many people see the policeman with a club in his hand and a gun on his hip out knocking down bad people and you just don't see a woman in this role. It all goes back to history. The evolution of law enforcement is now changing, though, from the punitive approach to prevention (7).

> I think she is confronted with two primary obstacles. One is the image that she carried with her to the public and that is from TV and what have you, depicting the policewoman as a half-masculine, half-feminine individual and the public's reaction is quite surprising when they meet a policewoman. We have tried not to present that image in anyway and they are, therefore, favorably surprised when they finally meet us. And secondly, there is the obstacle of working with the male officers. So many have ingrained feelings regarding females in the department, primarily because of the equal pay status, and they feel that they're out in the patrol car exposed to greater hazards than we are and we're so much more protected and they feel this really isn't equal. We don't do equal work so we shouldn't receive equal pay . . . I feel I've had to work doubly hard to prove myself on various assignments (18).

The stereotype image of the woman police officer was mentioned again and again by various policewomen. It is felt that the public possesses this image of the policewoman as a "bull dyke," or super-masculine woman officer who goes around belting people. As already mentioned in Chapter 3, Alice Stebbins Wells was described in this way by many newspapers in 1910! Amazing, the power of the media to create or to amplify stereotypes and have people accept them. And, of course, when speaking of the public, it must be remembered that the future male police officers are socialized by these stereotypes from their infancy. Then women themselves fall prey to this stereotyped thinking of their own capabilities and the roles that are "correct" for them to fill. What happens when a male police chief and a woman sergeant do not overcome their upbringings which have taught them the traditional rules and behavior for men and women in our society? A Los Angeles Police Department female officer comments:

> Right now, in this department, the biggest problem confronting the policewoman is the administration. We have an administration now which feels that police work is a man's job . . . I really don't think that the chief feels that policewomen are ineffective, but I think he doesn't feel that a woman's place is in police work because it's just a dirty job and it hardens many policewomen . . . I don't think the chief is down on women really but I think his reasoning is that women should maintain their femininity and this is not the place to do it because, for women, this is a hard job (10).

The key point in the preceding statement, though, is that it is just as difficult for men not to become cynical and dehumanized as it is for women who become police officers. As Niederhoffer pointed out, cynicism and quite often alienation are discernible at all levels and in every branch of law enforcement.[17] Men and women are both susceptible to this, but there are many officers of both sexes who are able to maintain a stable, emotional outlook on life and not let their jobs kill their spirit. The author does not mean to imply that all policemen have negative attitudes towards policewomen. Male officers take both sides of the issue. But a substantial number of male officers have strongly impeded and resisted women in law enforcement. This resistance takes on many different shapes and forms, but the basic reason behind the resistance is that the male with a job and power feels threatened by the female who wants the same things. Therefore, he resists her attempts to acquire them. The male defensive mechanisms range from the irrational to the rational. The irrational male responses encompass blatant and overt discrimination, as well as subtle and snide jokes and comments toward policewomen. These responses toward women in law enforcement are projected by the ordinary male officer who objects to a policewoman getting the same salary as a male and the top administrator who feels that women cannot preserve their femininity in police work. Somewhat more rational arguments against the use of policewomen are presented as the female's lack of physical capability and versatility as compared with that of the male officer's.*

The attitudes of policewomen are split concerning their role in law enforcement. Some of the older female officers perceive their role as it always has been, working with females and juveniles. They feel that they can do meaningful and effective work in this area because of their expertise and because male officers do not consider this "real" police work. Of course selfish motives probably lie behind the reluctance of some policewomen to see their role changed. These women are considered specialists with prestige jobs and good working hours, so perhaps their reluctance to change is understandable. Policewomen hired within the last several years have been used on some departments in a wider range of tasks, though. They perceive themselves as more generalist than specialist and seek to change the role of policewomen in that direction.

This dichotomy of attitudes among policewomen is evidenced in the definition of a policewomen in the opening of this chapter. Although this definition was formulated in 1966 at a workshop of policewomen, it still is evidence of the split today. The definition describes a policewoman being "appointed for the increased moral protection of women and minors and for the prevention of delinquency among such women and minors, and for such other police duties as can best be performed by a woman." Many policewomen who accept this part of the definition advocate separate women's bureaus, too. Other policewomen, not clear about the "duties that can best be performed by a woman," do not advocate separate bureaus but call for the complete integration of the policewoman throughout the police department.

Of course community attitudes have influenced male and female attitudes and vice versa. Just as the male and female attitudes about policewomen are mixed, so too is the community attitude (as a

*Both of these areas will be discussed later in the book.

whole) varied. On the one hand, some very positive statements and feelings about policewomen exist. Many male and female citizens react favorably to a policewoman and her "softer" image. On the other hand, many members of the public feel that women should not be in police work or used only to a limited extent. Aside from stereotyped thinking concerning "correct" male and female roles, one of the causes of the community's ambiguity is just the lack of knowledge about the woman police officer. The public generally has the "bull dyke" image of a policewoman and tends to think that the only work she performs is with juveniles and female prisoners. Mass media has helped to distort the realistic picture of police work in the public's mind to one of blood and gunfights and "Dirty Harrys." Further, the public thinks that police work is a man's work, and it is not aware of, nor has it been exposed to, the vast area of law enforcement where policewomen can be and have been effective.

REFERENCES

1. Theresa M. Melchionne, "Report of Committee 'A' Organization and Administrative Considerations," *Proceedings of Workshop for Policewomen,* (Eds.) Nelson A. Watson and Robert N. Walker (Washington, International Association of Chiefs of Police, 1966), p. 1.
2. Theresa M. Melchionne, "Current Status and Problems of Women Police," *The Journal of Criminal Law, Criminology and Police Science,* LVIII (June 1967), 257-260.
3. Eisenberg, D.A. Kent and E.R. Wall, *Police Personnel Practices in State and Local Governments* (Washington, Police Foundation, December 1973), pp. 11, 34.
4. Eisenberg, Kent and Wall, *Police Personnel Practices in State and Local Governments,* p. 19.
5. *Ibid,* pp. 18-19.
6. Catherine Milton, *Women in Policing* (Washington, Police Foundation, 1972), p. 17.
7. Norval Morris and Gordon Hawkins, *The Honest Politician's Guide to Crime Control* (Chicago, University of Chicago Press, 1970), p. 93.
8. Milton, *Women in Policing,* p. 40.
9. Eisenberg, Kent and Wall, *Police Personnel Practices in State and Local Governments,* p. 34.
10. Milton, *Women in Policing,* p. 40.
11. Melchionne, "Current Status and Problems," p. 260.
12. Milton, *Women in Policing,* p. 19.
13. Melchionne, "Report," p. 3.

14. Milton, *Women in Policing*, p. 20.
15. Eleanore L. Hutzel, *The Policewoman's Handbook* (Worcester, Columbia University Press, 1933), pp. 2-3.
16. Melchionne, "Report," p. 46.
17. Arthur Niederhoffer and Abraham S. Blumberg (Eds.), *The Ambivalent Force: Perspectives on the Police* (Waltham, Ginn and Company, 1970), p. 179.

CHAPTER 5

POLICEWOMEN OUTSIDE OF GENERAL PATROL

AFTER DISCUSSING the various obstacles confronting women in law enforcement, where should policewomen be utilized? Should policewomen be used only in certain areas of police work and not in others? In this chapter the author does not wish to consider the question of whether women can and/or should perform the uniformed, general patrol function on police departments. Because this question will be most ambiguous and difficult to resolve, it will need an in-depth examination; however, there are vital and necessary tasks which have to be done by police officers outside of general patrol. So while the general patrol function remains the primary *raison d'être* of police agencies, they could not possibly be successful in protecting and serving the community without officers acting competently in staff and auxiliary capacities. On some departments this encompasses a substantial number of personnel. As much as 50 to 60 percent of the sworn police personnel on various large and medium sized police departments perform tasks outside of general patrol. Even on small police agencies, officers specialize in nonpatrol duties.

Where then, and in what capacity, should policewomen be used? In the same way that male officers are used? Two female officers comment on this:

My true feeling is that women are suited for all areas of law enforcement. Let's take, for example, the problem of a disturbance call which is one of the most frequent calls that field officers handle. Now, initially, when that call comes into the station, they don't know whether it's a family disturbance thing or a little gambling beef or a two-neighbor

48

disturbance, it's just a disturbance. Until recently, they had never re-searched or tried to send women on any of these calls. Very recently, New York City Police started a "Family Crisis Unit" where they took some men and women and trained them in the skills and knowledges of other disciplines such as psychology, sociology, et cetera, in order to better handle disturbance calls. They found that the presence of a woman officer at a family disturbance between husband and wife rather calms the male and the woman officer has empathy more toward another woman and can get to the bottom of the beef, and they [the police unit] are able to handle this call the first time and not have to come back to handle it again, which is the case so often. So a woman can be valuable there. In any type of detection work where it is more a matter of mental ability than physical prowess (13).

In every aspect of law enforcement, there is a place for women. If, in the patrol station, it's not out in the black and white [patrol car], they can certainly do the job in the station. We have to have a woman in there for female prisoners. We use the girls at the complaint desk and they give out the calls. We have women juvenile officers at each station so if there is any problem in the field, a woman can be sent right out to the field. In every aspect, there is a place for women. I'm not saying that every job can be filled by a woman but in every large part of law enforcement, there is a place for them (15).

With the exception of the general patrol function, most of the policewomen spoken to by the author want to see women utilized in any and every job, and they feel that a woman can do just as competent a job as any man.

Historically and today still, policewomen have been hired mostly to work in the nonpatrol areas. The primary jobs exist in the juvenile area, searching females, and perhaps investigating certain crimes where females are victims or suspects and the secretarial role. So using women in these spots is nothing new. Policewomen in these positions perform necessary functions, though, which would have to be done by some department employee. One has to question the validity of having a trained officer as a secretary, however. With the shortage of sworn officers available to most departments, it behooves the police administrator to get the most meaningful performances out of all his officers. If the top administrator does not employ policewomen in valid, worthwhile jobs, he wastes their time and skills, as well as the department's budget money, because civilian clerks can be hired at half the cost of policewomen. There is no sense in hiring and training and paying a good salary to a female officer if all she is going to do is perform in a clerical capacity. A trend has developed in the nation's police departments to hire civilian employees to perform noncritical tasks, thereby freeing male officers to perform patrol duties or other necessary functions. This trend must also include the female officer in order to utilize her most effectively. Two policewomen express their feelings about this and other areas:

> I think they [policewomen] ought to relieve the men to go out in the field, like desk sergeants in the station, booking procedures except in the case where there is a man who is hostile. Administration, detectives, even in patrol, a woman could be in a car with a male. A lot of women don't want to because they're afraid of what might happen as valid somewhat about women but here is the thing. A lot of times a man will ride alone in a car so what is the difference if he is riding alone or he has a woman with him? I don't say she ought to go out and hassle crooks by herself but a guy wouldn't do it by himself. He'd get a backup unit, anyway (2).

> Practically all areas of law enforcement are suitable for policewomen. I think the woman should be out in a patrol car periodically. I think it looks good and it softens the present image that we seem to have now of law enforcement. I think that women should be used all over but I really don't agree with the current trends. I agree to a point in the current trend of utilizing the women officers in a greater area than they've ever been used before. The theory behind it, I understand, is to put more men out in the field and put us into some of the more clerical-type jobs that have been done by male officers in the past. This is fine, again, to a point; however, there are many jobs that I think we do as law enforcement officers (both men and women) that could be very easily done by clerical staff or civilian employees. I'd like to see policewomen get out and do more law enforcement work. All the stations should have female juvenile officers and I think there is a definite need for female detectives, as well (22).

Policewomen were initially hired in America and in most countries of the world to deal with juveniles of both sexes when they came in contact with police agencies either as runaways from home or victims or perpetrators of crime. One female officer comments about the traditional use of policewomen in the juvenile area. Here again, another stereotype of women and the types of jobs they should do (according to society's standards) is indicated:

> There is this built-in thing that automatically because a woman is a female that she should be able to work juvenile. There are some

women who like it and do well in it. But some women can do and have done work in areas such as organized crime or whatever but they're limited because the people are set with such an idea that you should only be able to deal with children so you stay here (in juvenile), and they are not getting the most utilization out of women officers. I do not think that women should be used in all areas of law enforcement, though, because, praise God, there is a difference and there are areas that man's expertise is necessary and a woman could never acquire (19).

Many women were hired by police departments just to search females taken into custody by male officers. In some departments these women carry the title "jail matrons," have no powers of arrest, receive no training and a small salary. Many other agencies, though, use their sworn policewomen in this capacity for several reasons. The administrators feel that they do not want to hire additional personnel or that not enough of a female prisoner problem exists to justify a jail matron. Again, a police administrator must ask himself the question if he is getting his "money's worth" by using a trained, skilled policewoman in a civilian, jail matron capacity. Having female officers perform jail matron duties in the station house also creates some problems for the field patrol officer when he confronts or arrests a female suspect. A female officer comments:

So, I don't see any reason why a woman shouldn't be assigned to each shift from each station to ride in a patrol car to respond to any incidents where there is a woman. Right now, officers in the field have to either detain female suspects and have a policewoman or matron come out and search them or take them down to the station to be searched by a policewoman or matron. The criminal element is not used to having women police officers handling them out in the field. And a lot of times, if they're stopped and they have something, they'll give it to the woman because they figure the male cop isn't going to search her and if they had a woman officer out in the field, she could prevent this (12).

Even when performing the general patrol function, a need still exists for woman officers out in the field as female and juvenile criminality increases. Female criminals cannot be effectively searched by male officers because of numerous prohibitions (mostly social ones not legal ones) against it. Female officers are needed in the field to search and question female criminals at the scene of the crime. Sheriff Pitchess of the Los Angeles County Sheriff's Department noted a startling increase in the number of females, both adult and juvenile, arrested in 1970 by his department. Pitchess pointed out that adult female arrests were up 23 percent—as opposed to a 10 percent increase in adult males arrested—and the increase of juvenile female arrests was twelve times greater than for male juveniles. While Sheriff Pitchess did not attribute this trend to any specific factor or movement, he did point out:

> Numerous sociological studies of female criminality have predicted that the female crime rate would approach male criminal rates as they achieve greater freedom and equality with males. As women emerge from their traditional role as housewife and mother, entering the political and business fields previously dominated by males, there is no reason to believe that women will not also approach equality with man in the criminal activity field.[1]

This trend occurs nationally as well, as evidenced by the FBI crime statistics. This increase in female criminality occurs not only in minor crimes but also in serious felonies. When serious crimes as a group are considered, arrests of males from 1967 to 1972 went up eighteen percent while female arrests increased 72 percent.[2]

Policewomen have been used and are being used today both in the United States and in foreign countries as detectives, decoys and plainclothes officers. Several policewomen interviewed felt that a good police administrator could use to his advantage some of the traditional attitudes that one associates with women, i.e. soft, non-aggressive, passive, when employing policewomen. Also, criminals do not look for female police officers.

> I think women could be used a lot more in detective and undercover work for the simple fact that people don't associate women with police work. They can get by with a lot more than two men walking into a bar. If a woman walks in or a man and woman walk in, all of a sudden they don't associate them as police officers. Then the stereotype that people have of women works to the policewoman's advantage (21).

> Women should be used in the investigative divisions much more so than they are used now. Even though they're good with juveniles, there is a good place for them in such crimes as forgery or embezzlement. Women participate in these crimes more. Women are so often the victims of sex crimes that women officers should be used in that area. Women officers can be used, of course, with juveniles and public relations (7).

I've made some good arrests as a detective because males just don't think a "broad" can be a cop. You can walk into places and work undercover as a female where male agents would be spotted in a minute by a crook. And of course there are just some investigations that have to be handled by a female. I don't care how slender and cute a male cop you dress up as a female for decoy work, he just isn't going to "make it" in most cases (17).

The author can only concur with the last statement, as will anyone else who has observed most male officers trying to act, move and look like a female for decoy assignments.

Another female officer comments about how the alleged characteristics of women can work to her advantage:

I feel that women can work in all areas of police work except for one-person patrol units. Three key areas where policewomen should be used more is in public relations, dealing with family disturbances and on the front desk of any police station. These areas are handled very effectively by women because of her, perhaps shall we say, softness and more understanding approach to a problem than many male officers have. Understanding and gentleness, coupled with knowledge and proper training, enable women officers to work in these types of areas very effectively (16).

Specific patrol refers to the concept of using officers (usually in plain clothes) in unmarked vehicles to deal with certain crimes and problem areas, such as juvenile gangs, sex crimes, burglaries and others.

One woman on the Los Angeles Police Department relates her experiences working in a field juvenile patrol car with a male partner. This indicates somewhat the feasibility and effectiveness of women in specific patrol units. But, although the juvenile cars proved effective, the top administrators decided that women should not be in the field.

I enjoyed the "J-car." If there was anything on this department I really liked, it was the "J-car." I had about six different male partners when I worked it for over one year. And of them, only one didn't care to work with a woman partner. All the rest liked it and enjoyed it. We knew each other's limitations and we never had any trouble working it. I never had any encounter where it was too much for either one of us to handle. We even had a few burglaries go down right in front of us and we got in on the initial start, and had no problems . . . I don't think one-man, one-woman in a general patrol car is too good but for a specific patrol like the "J-car," it's great. I think they should bring back the juvenile car because we were out there for the specific reason of juveniles and that is what we worked on, and we had the problem licked at the bus depots and places where they hang out. And now the patrol car doesn't have time to check these areas and the juvenile problems are big there again. They stopped juvenile patrol because some one "upstairs" felt that they didn't want women in the car. Never had any accidents, or injuries or any trouble; just somebody decided that they didn't want it. We have turmoil in our department! It worked and I saw it work, and I think we should have it again to handle the immense male and female juvenile crime problems (5).

Conclusion

Leaving aside the area of general patrol, where, then, can policewomen best be utilized? Women officers can and should be used in all major facets of police work, even in the field. If some police administrators feel that a policewoman would not be effective in a general patrol situation, she still should work as a detective in undercover and decoy work or in specific patrols such as juvenile and sex crimes. The resourceful police chief can exploit the fact that most people today do not think that an "average" looking woman could be a police officer. Several one-man, one-woman units would be valuable to have out in the field. These units could deal with the increased number of female criminals, as well as the female and juvenile victims of crime. As mentioned elsewhere by the first policewomen quoted in this chapter, female officers prove very effective on family disturbance calls, and these field units could be assigned these type of calls, too.

The female officer can also be used in many of the vital and necessary "inside" (the police station) tasks that are required in a police agency, thereby freeing males for street work. Such tasks as community relations, juvenile, communications, traffic analysis and others have to be performed by police officers. Policewomen should not be relegated to a supporting (quasi-civilian) role in law enforcement, but the tasks they can effectively perform are as important and necessary as the field patrol officer's. Perhaps policewomen cannot work effectively in all areas of police work, but numerous positions exist where the only qualification for the job should be the individual's capability to competently perform the job rather than the individual's sex. As a coda to this chapter, a female officer comments:

A lot of women know they can do a job and they feel they can do the job and use their brain power instead of being restricted to a few certain divisions where women have been traditionally assigned. We think we can go into other things where you don't need your brawn, you just need your brains (13).

REFERENCES

1. Peter Pitchess, "Startling Increase in Female Criminality" (Los Angeles, Los Angeles County Sheriff's Information Bureau, April 20, 1971). Mimeographed.
2. Federal Bureau of Investigation, *Uniform Crime Reports*, 1972, p. 34.

CHAPTER 6

GENERAL PATROL

THIS CHAPTER might be the most controversial chapter in the book for several reasons, for the question of whether or not females can perform general patrol duties will be examined. This question touches directly on the heart of the whole matter concerning the usage of women in law enforcement. Many people feel that police work is a dangerous and violent profession; women as the "weaker sex" would not be able to handle dangerous and violent situations effectively. People also feel that general patrol is the primary function of a police department to which the majority of personnel are assigned and that danger and violence are most frequently encountered by the patrol officer. Even many male and female supporters of current and/or increased utilization of policewomen draw the line when the issue of putting females in general patrol units arises. They feel that the policewoman proves valuable and necessary in many areas of law enforcement but not in field patrol. These areas, examined in the previous chapter, are mostly inside (the police station) tasks and relatively safe when compared to the patrol officer's job. Of course, many police administrators of medium- and small-sized police agencies feel that they cannot afford the luxury of specialists and that every officer on their department has to be a generalist and be capable of performing general field patrol duties even if he is a part-time specialist. Many of these administrators resist the utilization of policewomen altogether, feeling that since she cannot effectively handle general patrol, she is not as valuable to the department in terms of versatility as a male would be.

The remainder of this chapter will examine several areas in an effort to reach a conclusion about the question of policewomen in general patrol.

The Foreign Experience

Chapter 2 looked at the historical and present employment of women on police agencies in various countries around the world. The author's purpose in this section is not to reiterate that chapter but to emphasize the performance of policewomen in general patrol and other hazardous and violent duties. American police agencies concerned with the issue of employing policewomen in general patrol would do well to examine and remember the successful work of women in general patrol on some foreign nations' police forces.

Of the countries discussed in Chapter 2, Great Britain, Japan, Guyana, Israel, and New Zealand all have policewomen performing general patrol duties. They have been used in this capacity for varying lengths of time, but in all of these nations the female officer has performed as well as the male officer on patrol, and the future will probably see increased numbers of policewomen on patrol. All of the policewomen in these countries receive, of course, proper training in self defense tactics and carry firearms with the exception of Great Britain where most male and female officers do not carry them. The policewomen in the aforementioned countries also function as detectives, criminal intelligence operatives, undercover agents in drug and vice situations and traffic officers. Female officers in these tasks face hazards, and the potential for violence is as great as, if not greater than, that encountered by general patrol officers.

West Germany has recently started to place female officers in detective positions. France, a country employing female officers to a very limited extent, has had females operating undercover in drug and vice situations where the hazards for the agent if exposed are enormous. Sweden has female officers in criminal investigation and criminal intelligence capacities.

Of course, female general patrol officers and females performing other hazardous and violent tasks have had their share of injuries and even deaths in the line of duty. But they have not been injured or killed any more or less than policemen. They have proved that they can successfully perform in violent, hazardous field patrol and other duties. The author realizes that general patrol and policing in general is not the same (in whatever country we are talking about) as in the United States. The general patrol function differs in foreign countries in several ways and for a number of reasons. But the successful foreign experience with policewomen in general patrol should not be lightly dismissed by American police administrators as not being applicable to American law enforcement. American police agencies have learned and adapted a number of concepts and innovations from foreign police over the years; now it is time to analyze and survey the foreign policewomen's performance and put whatever is applicable to good use here in America.

The American Experience

Although some other countries have employed policewomen on general patrol and in other hazardous assignments for a number of years, various American police agencies now do this as well.

The Indianapolis Police Department has placed females in general patrol units since 1968. Car 47 is a two-female patrol unit on the street during the day and evening shifts, seven days a week. This unit handles the whole range of police calls, but they are often dispatched to the scene of family fights and disturbances. The female and male officers on the force have not had any special training for handling family crises, but the policewomen in Car 47 have proved particularly successful in dealing with this type of call. An older Indianapolis patrolman commented, "There are some families that when they get going will call you back two or three times a night. But I notice that when the women go, that is the last time we hear from them."[1] Five females on the force work as plainclothes narcotics officers, exposed to hazardous violent situations as part of their job. Of course, all the policewomen in field positions on the department call for assistance when it is needed, but they have not had to do so any more or less than policemen in field positions.

The Miami Police Department has four policewomen on general patrol duty in two-officer units with male or female partners. These officers handle the whole range of calls assigned to patrol units. Six female traffic officers handle accidents and accident investigations and usually patrol in one-officer units. Nine other female criminal investigators operate with or without a partner as the situation demands. These police women in traffic and detective positions face dangerous situations; still they have performed satisfactorily.

The Peoria Police Department has seven policewomen in general patrol, one-officer units. One policewoman in a patrol unit, Officer Marcella Daniels, feels that being a woman enables her to be more effective than a male patrol officer in certain situations. In 1972, two male officers had a tough time convincing a female who was threatening to commit suicide not to do it. When Officer Daniels arrived, the woman, relieved to see another woman, abandoned her suicide attempt. Officer Daniels comments about another advantage she feels she has: "Most of the violent situations are family fights, and I find that if you can talk to people and calm them down they are a lot less likely to hit you."[2] Captain Gail Owens, Chief of Patrol, is an avid supporter of females in general patrol duty. He stated his original skepticism with the program but, "I couldn't be more pleasantly surprised at how well our girls are working out. They are good officers and they can do the job, I'm convinced."[3]

The New York City Police Department has female officers performing in all capacities and doing the whole range of police tasks that occurs on the world's largest police force. Policewomen work in dangerous and potentially violent jobs such as narcotics, detectives, criminal intelligence, and 400 of them are on general patrol with a partner, either on foot or in a patrol car. A successful year-long experiment with women on general patrol duty provided the impetus for putting more policewomen in patrol. This trend is resisted by some male officers and the powerful Patrolmen's Benevolent Association, but women in patrol perform well.

The St. Louis County Police Department employs approximately 20 policewomen on general patrol. St. Louis County ranks third behind New York and Washington in the number of women officers utilized on general patrol duty. The department has just finished a year-long evaluation of these officers. Although the finalized written study has not been completed yet, the author has been in touch with the head of this study, Dr. Lewis Sherman of the University of Missouri at St. Louis. The findings of this study will show that the policewomen have performed as well as policemen with the same amount of time and experience in field patrol work. The policewomen in patrol have performed successfully; there is no reason to believe that they will not continue to do so in the future.[4] The interesting thing about the County's utilization of policewomen in patrol and this study is that all patrol officers work in one-person patrol vehicles. The other two major studies concerning women in patrol in Washington, D. C. and New York City evaluated the

policewoman's field work with partners present. One-person patrol units are hazardous and the potential for violence is always present when a lone officer gets involved in any type of situation. Back-up, assistance units are usually some distance away in St. Louis County, so the officer has to be intelligent and sure of herself when she handles a call. Of course, as one County policewoman commented, "Some field situations can't be handled by a female or male officer alone. Back-up units have to be called to insure officer safety."[5] This study will probably be most pertinent for police administrators of medium- and small-sized departments to look at to evaluate the question of policewomen on patrol on their departments.

The Washington, D. C. Police Department has female officers in virtually every aspect of police work, including over 150 on general patrol. As mentioned in Chapter 3, a preliminary study of the policewomen's performance, based on four months' patrol duty, has already been published and released. A year-long continuation study of policewomen on patrol has just been completed, but it has not yet been published or released to the public. The author would like to provide the reader some of the findings of the preliminary study, as these will provide a definite insight as to what the findings of the continuation study will be. Some of the highlights of the study are:

Forty-seven percent of the women have made one or more felony arrests, compared to 61 percent of the men. On the average, new women made fewer misdemeanor arrests and gave fewer moving traffic violations than the comparison male. (However, a substantial number of women participated in as many or more arrests or traffic citations as the typical male.) Before the arrest figures can be used as valid indices of performance, however, the authors caution that follow-up work will have to determine how well arrests hold up in court.

Although the new policewomen and the new men (in the comparison group) were involved in few situations involving violence or potential violence, there appeared to be no difference in their performance in those few situations; however, policemen, policewomen and officials all agree that fewer women than men can handle violent or potentially violent situations satisfactorily. The women think less difference exists between women and men than do the men.

Police service given by patrolmen and patrolwomen proves equally acceptable to citizens.

New women were more likely than new men to be given instructions by their partner and were less likely to take charge at an incident in which their partner was present.

Before the experiment began, policemen expressed considerable opposition to the idea of women as patrol officers because they expected the women to make their own jobs more difficult. Working with women has not had much effect on the men's attitudes, although the negative feelings are much less pronounced among younger officers and black officers. The authors speculate that these attitudes may have made the new women's jobs somewhat more difficult.

Male officers seemed to experience much less favorable public response than the females. Males perceived the public as less cooperative, and they reported receiving 50 percent more insults and close to three times as many threats or attempts at injury, with less than half the compliments, as the women reported.

All the women still in the department are expected to be recommended for retention at the end of their probationary year.[6]

The basic findings of this preliminary study show that policewomen on patrol duty perform as well as men. From these findings, though, several areas should be examined and surely the continuation study will do so. But whatever the differences and questions (i.e. why the disparity between female and male arrest rates?) concerning the policewomen on patrol, the author feels that they all can be traced back to three things: training, newness on the job and male resistance. Perhaps training has to be upgraded or modified to some extent. The problem of newness and not having any successful female models to emulate will be overcome by time and experience and as policewomen make good arrests and get promoted. Male resistance to policewomen on patrol will take longer to overcome and will probably be overcome only by successful female job performance and more young males getting into positions of authority. It is the author's opinion, based on the preliminary study, that the continuation study of policewomen on patrol in Washington,

D. C., will find that females can do the job and should do the job in general patrol.*

Women in Other Hazardous Jobs

It is interesting to look at some other professions besides police work, where women are employed in order to get a better perspective about whether women can handle danger and violence. These other jobs have just as many, if not more, hazards as police work and often have more potential for violent confrontations than general patrol duty.

The first hazardous occupation examined is part of the criminal justice system—corrections. Ever since males and females were placed in separate correctional institutions in America, the female correctional officer has had to handle and supervise female prisoners. This role has placed the female correctional officer's safety in jeopardy numerous times at various institutions, but she has handled herself well in overcoming violent situations. In recent years a trend emerged towards militancy and violence on a mass scale in our nation's prisons. This trend has not escaped female institutions, so the female correctional officer has also faced large-scale hazards and violence at times. Just recently, primarily because of a shortage of qualified male officers, a number of all-male prisons have hired females for guard positions. Female correctional officers serve presently in such institutions as Louisiana State Prison (Angola), New Jersey State Prison at Trenton, State Prison of Southern Michigan at Jackson and San Quentin Prison. Most of the female officers at all-male prisons work with perimeter and external security of the prison, but all are on call to deal with any violent and dangerous situation at the prison administrator's direction.

Female nurses and other staff have worked in female mental institutions for many years. There they have had to handle violence which, at its worst, gives the patient (female or male) "superhuman" strength. Within the last ten to fifteen years, the utilization of female nurses and aides has extended to male mental institutions as well. And it seems that one advantage females have over male

*The Police Foundation has recently reported that the continuation study of policewomen on patrol in Washington indicates that there is no significant difference in job performance between male and female officers on patrol duty. Also, there was no difference in their ability to handle violent or potentially violent situations.

nurses and aides is their calming effect on male patients prone to violence. Dr. Milton Greenblatt, Commissioner of Massachusetts Department of Mental Health, stated that "female nurses on male wards, even on very disturbed wards, usually have a good effect on the anger, belligerence, and violent tendencies . . . For this reason, many 'disturbed' wards do have female attendants and nurses on them and now this concept has been generally accepted and widely applied throughout mental hospitals in the nation."[7] This pacifying quality that women have (more so than men) is a vital asset in police work. Another example of this female quality was observed in a St. Louis housing project.

Several years ago the University of Missouri at St. Louis (UMSL) received a grant to train 150 residents of the public housing projects in St. Louis as unarmed security guards. These guards received training more in crisis intervention than crime control in a 240-hour training program, as they did not replace St. Louis Police officers, only supplemented them. Four women became security guards at the Pruitt-Igoe housing project reputed to be one of the most dangerous in the country. The women went on patrol with male or female partners, as the work schedule called for, to handle all types of complaints from tenants. According to Dr. Sherman of UMSL who directed the training program, the female guards performed as well as male guards, and the only difference was that they evoked a different (favorable) response from residents than male guards.[8] In a letter to Catherine Milton of the Police Foundation, Dr. Sherman comments:

> The special abilities of the women are numerous. First, they clearly emphathize with the plight of a woman who calls for assistance in a family crisis. The male guards, on the other hand, not only fail to appreciate the woman's position, but very often will give covert or even overt support and encouragement to the aggression of the male. The male guards frequently exacerbate conflict rather than resolve it. The residents see this distinctly and are keenly aware of the compassion and understanding a woman brings when responding to their call of distress.
>
> Another factor and probably the most important one, is that men by their attitudes and behavior frequently elicit more anger and violence in a family crisis situation; the women tend to defuse potentially violent situations by their intervention style. Since the four women at Pruitt-Igoe are big, aggressive and quite formidable in appearance,

some other, more subtle psychological factors are involved in eliciting hostility.[9]

Of course, females have successfully performed other dangerous and potentially violent jobs for years. Many female nurses and aides work in metropolitan hospital emergency rooms where wounded, deranged and combative patients are often encountered. Another fact to keep in mind when wondering if females can handle dangerous and violent situations is that in various societies and at various times throughout history, female warriors and soldiers have fought and died in battle.

All of this experience in foreign police agencies, in various American police agencies and in other hazardous jobs makes it plain that the most common reason for excluding females from general patrol —"It's too violent and dangerous a job for females"—may not be true. Women can effectively handle whatever risk and danger exists in general patrol duty. Of course, just as policemen call for assistance in hazardous situations, so will the policewomen, so seldom will she be facing danger and violence alone. But a key factor to examine in determining whether women can handle the danger and violence of patrol duty is just exactly how dangerous and violent patrol is.

Violence and Patrol

Anyone examining this question of how violent patrol is will probably be surprised at the answer. For police work is not as violent as people perceive it to be. Officer Daniels of the Peoria police comments, "It's not surprising that a woman can do a patrol job because 85 percent of police calls are service calls, reports of accidents, deaths and assaults, and only 15 percent are actually violent action when police get there. There is more need for brain than brawn."[10] The reader may question the 85 percent figure cited by Officer Daniels; however, various time/work studies done in a number of cities show that the average patrol officer spends anywhere from 80 to 95 percent of his tour of duty handling various service-type calls (i.e. calling ambulances, directing traffic, report writing) which are unrelated to crime control or law enforcement.[11] This percentage of service calls varies from community to community and by day of week and time, but basically the 80 to 95 percent range is valid.

When one looks at the dead and injured on the job rates of police work as compared to other occupations, it becomes clear that policing is not an especially dangerous job. In New York City, for instance, during the first nine months of 1966, firemen had three times more injuries and sanitation men four times more injuries than policemen. And in terms of the number of days off for each injury, the injuries suffered by firemen and sanitation men were more serious than those suffered by policemen.[12] The death rate for policing is relatively small when compared with a number of other common occupations. Underground mining is almost three times as dangerous as policing, construction work is more than twice as dangerous and agriculture is about one and one-half times as dangerous. Of course, policemen are killed in the line of duty, but until the last few years, the rate of policemen killed had been falling for the past fifty years.[13]

Why then do many people perceive police work as being violent with just one episode of mayhem after another? There are several reasons. One of them perhaps was obvious to the reader when looking at the death and injury rates of policing as compared to other occupations. The element of human intention to kill or injure enters into police work as opposed to the accidental nature of deaths and injuries in most other occupations. This element of human intention in police deaths and injuries has led to the police and the public being very acutely aware of violence directed at police officers. Of course, the media, particularly television and cinema, has distorted the hazards and violence in police work completely out of proportion. The public tends to think that police work involves just one fight or shoot-out after another. On television 1973-1974 has to be the "year of the cop" (of course, only the male cop) and also in the cinema and in the books of America. It is truly amazing the amount of violence and death related to policing in the media. All the shots fired on one week's television shows by police officers would probably exceed the amount of shots fired by the whole New York City Police Department in a year's time. And police officers do not escape from this perception of police work as violent. Many police officers, especially recruits and rookies, do have this same distorted picture of policing as the general public. Policemen see the media's presentation of police work, and it is very glamorous and action packed, not boring, tedious and often mundane like real police work. So as they consciously or unconsciously adopt some of this "action" into their own perception of policing, they start to think of themselves as "Dirty Harrys." This type of perception about the violence and hazards of police work receives constant reinforcement in the officer's mind by recruit and in-service training where violence and officer safety is constantly discussed.

Even if there is less danger and violence to police work than imagined, there still is some degree of it. The reason behind the feeling that policewomen should not be in general patrol is that they are not strong enough to handle dangerous and potentially violent situations even if only 1 percent of police work falls into this category. It is interesting to note, though, that most police departments make no effort to test the strength of anyone applying for a job. They really cannot say whether the males hired have the necessary strength. Strength or the lack of it is a moot point, though, in most dangerous situations. There is a strong tendency in police training to think that officer safety is manageable. Again, because of the human intention element involved in police injuries, one is inclined to believe that if only proper procedures were followed, proper precautions taken and if one were sufficiently alert and acute, danger and violence could have been abated. To some extent this is true. Proper training, procedures and alertness are necessary for officer safety. But ambush-type attacks killed fourteen police officers in 1972 and nineteen police officers in 1971. The International Association of Chiefs of Police (IACP) in a recent study of police fatalities and injuries commented, "The common denominator in all of the incidents has been the element of surprise. In almost every case the attack occurred while the victim was performing a routine function or simply sitting, standing, or walking. In many cases, the officer never even saw his assailant."[14]

Therefore, in many dangerous situations the question of the strength or sex of the officer is irrelevant since only clairvoyance can prevent death or injury. In other situations (besides ambush) that resulted in death, the IACP concluded that training and the ability to think clearly and quickly are more important than physical strength.[15] Properly trained female officers would not have any less ability than male officers to think clearly and quickly.

There are other potentially violent situations on general patrol duty where the officer definitely does influence the outcome of an encounter either positively or negatively. And whether or not violence occurs between the police and citizenry in different situations has much more to do with various psychological factors than the strength or the sex of the police officer at the scene. A social psychological phenomenon known as "the self-fulfilling prophecy" comes into play often in police-citizen contacts. This phenomenon has been observed and tested in a number of other areas outside police work, too. Basically the thought behind it is that our expectations of future events sometimes cause us to behave in ways that help bring about the events we expect.[16] As it pertains to police-citizen encounters, it means that a person's own attitude and appearance may provoke behavior that is not necessarily inherent in a situation. An officer who intervenes in a situation has the ability to change the course of action by his own attitudes and behavior. If the officer's attitudes and verbal and nonverbal communications are positive (i.e. peaceful, nonviolent), then the situation will probably end without aggression by either party even if the situation is one in which the citizen is arrested. On the other hand, if the officer's attitudes and verbal and nonverbal communications are negative (i.e. aggressive, threatening), then the situation will probably end with aggression by both parties.

This self-fulfilling prophecy, of course, also influences the citizen, often causing him to "provoke" violence toward the police officer, rather than the other way around. Citizens have reacted to their own perceptions and expectations of police behavior (not what actually occurred), thereby provoking violence. As Dr. Sherman points out in an interesting article, "Because there is only a thin line between entering the situation prepared for violence and entering the situation and eliciting violence, what a policeman may feel is the correct behavior for him may be perceived by a citizen as an invitation to aggression."[17]

Since perceptions and expectations are very influential in determining people's behavior, what would occur in different situations if policewomen were placed on general patrol duty? Before answering this, though, one has to keep in mind all the perceptions, expectations and stereotypes that Americans associate with either sex. Females are mild, lenient, sympathetic, understanding, compassionate and motherly. Males are stern, rugged, tough, hard, aggressive and patriarchal. Dr. Sherman comments, "Whether these stereotypes reflect present day reality is beside the point; our concern is with expectation, with the postulate upon which people base their predictions of other people's behavior."[18] American society expects women to be less hostile, less aggressive and less physical than men. Based upon these psychological and social factors, the effect of female nurses in male mental health wards and the experience of field policewomen in family disturbances* and other situations, it seems reasonable to expect that women on general patrol will arouse less antagonism, stimulate less fear and provoke less violence than patrolmen. Policewomen will have a greater calming effect on aggressive behavior and will also elicit less violence and abuse than policemen.[19]

This feminine capacity to dispel male anger may also be due in part to the value system of male criminals: assaults on male authority figures (the "cop") are ranked high. Policemen are often attacked "because it is heroic," says Ronald Talney of the Multnomah County, Oregon, Sheriff's Department. But policewomen might avoid such assaults simply because "it is cowardly to attack a woman, even though she is a police officer."[20] This effect would be even more pronounced when a policewoman is confronting an individual with his peer group present, for the loss of status within one's peer group would be a significant factor in controlling the individual's behavior.

Conclusion

|Properly selected, trained and supervised, policewomen can and should be doing the job of general patrol.\This chapter has touched on all the justifications which point to this conclusion. There is the successul foreign experience of placing women in field patrol. Although there are only (at the maximum) 900 policewomen on general patrol in the United States, they have performed well in communities as diverse as Bogalusa, Louisiana and New York City.

*One of the most hazardous and potentially violent situations for police in terms of the number of officers killed and injured each year in handling this type of call.

There is the good performance of women in other hazardous and potentially violent jobs. When general patrol is examined, it is not as violent or hazardous as most people think. Many instances of violence, though, in police work cannot be prevented by strength or anything else; it's just a matter of fate or "bad luck" when the officer's "number" comes up. And in the many situations where the police officer can influence the final outcome, the strength and sex of the officer are not as important as his/her attitudes and expectations.

Not all women can effectively function as general patrol officers. But the author feels that not all men can effectively function as general patrol officers, either. And perhaps these men and women who cannot be or do not want to be general patrol officers could still perform other departmental functions successfully. There has been talk in police circles in the last several years of incorporating private industry's concept of career paths into policing. Basically, this would create specialist or generalist, managerial or nonmanagerial career paths for employees to follow on a police department. This should give the organization and the employee maximum job performance and job satisfaction. But for police administrators who need generalists and view every police recruit as a prospective field officer, women can still do the job as generalists in patrol.

If a certain realistic level of strength and agility is tested for and found necessary for a patrol officer in order to fulfill his role, then women must be given the opportunity to take an exam which tests this. It is not the author's contention that men and women are physically alike. Aside from the very obvious differences between the sexes, there still is the basic fact that women (as a group) are not as strong as men (as a group). Women do have slower times in track and swimming contests and are not able to lift as much weight in weightlifting competition. This is due in part to the facts that women have less bone structure, less musculature, smaller lung capacity and less physical mass than males. But the question law enforcement has to examine is do we want officers who can bench-press two hundred pounds or run a mile in under five minutes? Are there factors which are more important for an officer to possess than this physical prowess? Aggressive and physical policing is not the final definition of good policing; good listening, compassionate understanding, and human responsiveness are equally important characteristics for all officers to possess. And again, to reiterate, if there is a physical level necessary for successful job performance, then let us test for it but let us test candidates of both sexes. Policewomen can perform general patrol duty as effectively as policemen, and they may in fact be able to perform it somewhat better.

REFERENCES

1. Catherine Milton, *Women in Policing* (Washington, Police Foundation, 1972), p. 65.
2. Milton, *Women in Policing*, p. 78.
3. Milton, *Women in Policing*, p. 80.
4. Statement by Dr. Lewis Sherman in personal interview, February 13, 1974.
5. Statement by anonymous St. Louis County Police officer in personal interview, January 1974.
6. Bloch, D. Anderson and P. Gervais, *Policewomen on Patrol*, vol. I (Washington, Police Foundation, February 1973), pp. 7-11.
7. Milton, *Women in Policing*, p. 30.
8. Lewis J. Sherman, "A Psychological View of Women in Policing," *Journal of Police Science and Administration* (December 1973), p. 388.
9. Milton, *Women in Policing*, p. 30.
10. Milton, *Women in Policing*, p. 78.
11. Arthur Niederhoffer and Abraham S. Blumberg (Eds.), *The Ambivalent Force: Perspectives on the Police* (Waltham, Ginn and Company, 1970), p. 177.
12. Ibid.
13. Rodney Stark, *Police Riots* (Belmont, Wadsworth Publishing Company, Inc., 1972), pp. 133-134.
14. Milton, *Women in Policing*, p. 27.
15. Ibid.
16. Sherman, "A Psychological View," p. 391.
17. Sherman, "A Psychological View," p. 392.
18. Ibid.
19. Ibid
20. *Time Magazine*, May 1, 1972, p. 60.

CHAPTER 7

SUPERVISION

THIS CHAPTER addresses itself to examining several questions concerning supervision as it relates to policewomen. Can a man supervise women? Can and should women be supervisors? Of men, too? These are all questions which have been on male administrators' minds for many years and in many other areas besides law enforcement. But private industry has answered these questions to a much greater extent than police agencies have. Just the fact that a greater percentage of female employees work in private security agencies rather than in public law enforcement agencies suggests this.

One key area of doubt which a police administrator might have is whether a female can supervise a male subordinate? Will a female supervisor have any special problems? Of course, these questions will be examined only by male administrators who accept the concept that women should be used in supervisory police positions at all. Most police officials feel that women should not be supervisors. Others feel that women should only supervise women. Then, only relatively few police executives and officers have accepted the concept of females supervising male subordinates.

Two female officers comment on their perspective of females supervising males in police departments:

> Women supervising women in, let's say a jail-type of supervision, is fine but women supervising men I don't think would be very logical. I just don't think it's in the scheme of things for a woman to supervise a man. I don't go for that myself. I couldn't comfortably supervise men. Personally, we (women) look to the man for leadership and everything, and I couldn't tell him what to do. I would if I had to and they said do it, but I wouldn't be comfortable (18).

There again, the role doesn't fit. Men are not made to be subjected to a woman. And they resent it, and I don't blame them. But, you see, you get a lot of attitudes from policewomen, "well I can do the job —I can do it as good or better than any man." Well that's the kind of an attitude that men resent, I think. So I really don't feel that women should be higher than sergeant (10).

Both of the preceding policewomen voice the traditional approach in their feeling that women should not be supervising men. The second respondent's comments prove very interesting since she herself is a sergeant. But she feels that women should only supervise women. Both of these women told the author that they were brought up from childhood to believe that man is the leader and woman is the follower in life. This kind of ingrained thinking as to what roles are proper in society for men and women must be overcome by both sexes in order to make the most effective use of policewomen.

I imagine there are special supervision problms until you're trained, again. You're always going to resent being told what to do by a woman. That's all through life. But private industry is meeting this. Private industry is working on it and is accomplishing it, and I think we (in law enforcement) can do it, too (7).

I think that if the supervisor is competent in her job I don't foresee any great problems that couldn't be overcome. I find that the better you are at your job and the more qualified you are, the more respect that you will gain. But I don't think this respect would be forthcoming immediately. I think it would have to be earned and I feel, again, that the woman has to work a little harder at this to develop this rapport and respect from subordinates. Much more so than say a male sergeant coming in and just taking over. But women can be good supervisors and we should be given a chance to show what we can do (28).

There are probably some problems that a female supervisor has but professionalism in police work will overcome this. By that, I mean that as the female supervisor becomes better trained to perform the job, then the problem will be negligible (14).

The three preceding policewomen feel that women can supervise men. At first, some resistance surfaces toward a new supervisor, but as she performs her job competently, she will be accepted by her subordinates. Proper training of both male and female supervisors and subordinates provides an important answer to whatever problems exist in the supervision area.

It's very hard for a male to accept orders from a woman. Normally, most of our female supervisors supervise other females. The few females that supervise males, though, haven't had many problems. Women could probably supervise in nonfield areas but you could never make her a supervisor in patrol because she doesn't have the experience and the patrolmen wouldn't accept her (23).

Many male police officers also feel this way. They feel that policewomen have had little or no field experience and thus would not be able to effectively supervise field officers. The males would not have the respect for her as a supervisor without her having prior field experience. That the female supervisor would not be "tough" enough with male subordinates is a feeling of some male officers, too.[1]

A female sergeant has some very incisive comments:

I feel that initially a woman supervisor would not be accepted. It would be like any new supervisor going into any unit. They're used to the old system, the old bosses. They've been able to relate to that supervision that was there. So that when you have a turnover, anyone new coming in has to gain everyone's confidence and has to show that she or he knows exactly the job and is willing to work with the group. But a woman, in this instance, if she had an all-male crew to do, she would have to not only win the respect, the confidence, she would have to show that she was trained and had the expertise for this particular assignment so they begin to accept her for her knowledge. But these are not just isolated to a woman; a man has this same thing. They would be looking more critically at a woman, though (18).

Aside from the fact that there will be a certain amount of male resistance and resentment toward female supervisors, policewomen can and should supervise women and/or men as their individual qualifications, training and expertise denote. While some males will totally be opposed to this change of traditional masculine and feminine roles in America, others will be only resentful and very critical of female supervisors. Women supervisors have had to work harder than male supervisors in order to prove themselves, but once they have shown that they know their jobs, the supervisors' subordinates have usually accepted their authority and position. As for female supervisors not being "tough" enough, if you properly train supervisors to handle subordinates, then they will be good supervisors (whether tough or not). Of course, the top police executive must support a female supervisor's valid actions just as he would a male supervisor's, otherwise her authority and responsibility become meaningless.

One valid criticism of female supervisors exists. A woman should not supervise a field-type unit if she has had no experience in the field. A supervisor (male or female) should have personal knowledge and experience of the field in order to effectively supervise field officers. Without this personal experience, certain problems and solutions to them may be overlooked by the supervisor, and he or she will probably not get the respect of subordinates. Many male field officers become just as resentful and critical of male supervisors who get promoted out of a "cushy" desk job and back into a uniformed, field, supervisory position for the very same reasons. To prevent a "Catch 22," though, if we agree that field supervisors need field experience, policewomen should be given the chance to be field officers and then, if they are competent, be promoted to field supervisory positions. Otherwise, they will be able to supervise only in certain specialized areas.

Perhaps a more basic question for police administrators to consider, since nearly all of the supervisory personnel in law enforcement are male, is can male administrators supervise female subordinates? Do males have any special problems supervising females? Some policewomen comment on their view of males supervising females:

> Male supervisors don't have any major problems with female subordinates. None at all (27).

> No more problems for male supervisors of females than there would be between male and male (16).

> Males can supervise females as long as they're firm and fair and don't play favorites (9).

So male police supervisors do not have any problems with female officers. Or do they? Some policewomen think that they do.

> Family situations are usually the big problem for male supervisors with female subordinates. Because a woman is generally responsible

for the care of the kids. When the kids are home sick, then she has to take off sick or if they have to go to the dentist, she has to take off to take them to the dentist. These types of things (10).

Male supervisors find it difficult to tell a woman about her personal appearance. If she is getting a little hefty, or a sloppy uniform appearance or has a hygiene problem, I have found that most men find this extremely difficult to talk to a woman about. Also, about their work. Men seem to be terribly afraid that if they yell at a woman, why she'll break down in tears and cry. They find this quite a distasteful encounter so they avoid it. And I don't think that's right because the male supervisor should supervise some women more closely. Some women are using their femininity like this. A lot of the men don't know that's what she'll do but they feel that she might do that so they avoid the situation and don't bring to her attention things that should be (2).

I've seen some women that have cried a little after being bawled out by a supervisor. Perhaps, women are more emotional than men in our society but this outward display of emotion shouldn't worry the male supervisor because after the woman is through crying, she goes right on and continues her job (11).

Family situations may cause some supervision problems for males with female subordinates. These are not that difficult to surmount, though. If a female has to take care of a certain family situation, then that person has to take a sick day or compensatory time off like any other employee. Female absenteeism and turn-over rates are not significantly different from male's. They will be discussed more thoroughly in Chapter 8. A more serious problem commented on appears to be a combination of a lack of effective and complete supervision of female subordinates by male supervisors. In turn the female subordinates use this ineffectiveness as a lever to achieve their own ends. The following policewoman indicates this:

A male supervisor has to be damn strong and damn sure of his own masculinity in regards to his being able to not be maneuvered by the female. Whereas, you can go on and tell another female that I can't come to work today because I have a cramp or something like that, you know. So the female supervisor would say, "well, I have them too, so bring it on in." The male would say, "I have empathy for you so don't come in." Or, she'll go through this bit with the tears, and he doesn't want to see that and she knows it, and so she throws it on his mind and in his presence. So he says, "hey, just get out of my way; you don't need to do that anymore, just get out of my way." And she has won her deal. If a male supervisor isn't sure of himself and can be maneuvered, he is also less apt to criticize females. And it's done (maneuvering) by women (9).

It appears that some women prefer male supervisors to female supervisors. And the reason is not that women are petty or cliquish or more emotional than men (however, this is partially true; women are allowed to show emotion where it is frowned upon for a man to show much emotion in America),[2] but the woman subordinate can and does maneuver many male supervisors for her own advantage. The following women sergeants had some very incisive comments on this and supervision in general:

> I'm sure there are problems that female supervisors have with male subordinates. I hear about some of them but to my face, I don't get many. I try to get along with them but I think there are a few of them that resent being told what to do by a woman. I, myself, have never had a big problem. I possibly have to be somewhat more diplomatic with males (26).

> I think most times women prefer to work for men. I guess they think the women supervisors are more fickle and demanding. I'm sure I'm probably more demanding than any of our other supervisors. I think this is the basis for most women preferring to work for men (26).

> I don't believe male supervisors have any special problems with women subordinates. See, we're getting down to the basics. I really believe that if you're trained, if you're qualified, I could care less if it was a female or male supervisor. Bad supervisors, male or female, have given bad names to the job (1).

It seems that male supervisors have not been trained to supervise women subordinates properly. Whatever training male supervisors have been given concerning female subordinates, it has usually been of the "don't scold her, send her 'get well' cards, be tactful" school of supervision. All this type of ineffective supervision leads to is problems. Any subordinate, male or female, will take advantage of a weak supervisor. If the supervisor proves remiss in his job and is afraid of the "emotional" woman, then the woman who so desires will turn this fear to her own advantage. Male police supervisors should be trained to effectively handle female subordinates. And the only training necessary is to tell the male supervisor to deal as firmly and effectively with women as they do with men subordinates. Women officers can handle the stress and rigors of police work because it has been proven many times. But poor supervision may lead to low quality work by subordinates.

This dual standard of supervision as adopted by many male supervisors towards male and female subordinates leads to other problems as well. A policewoman comments:

Some supervisors (male) have been overprotective of female officers in certain field situations. I think this has caused some grumbling by male officers (22).

Of course, it has. Male and female officers will perceive this overprotectiveness and lack of consistent discipline towards policewomen. This will cause male officers to resent females because they are "getting away with murder" and because they get the easy, less dangerous assignments. Female officers will begin to doubt themselves and their performance in field situations and perhaps, again, to manipulate their supervisor. Police Chief Wilson of Washington, D. C., had to issue a special memorandum to his officers and supervisors concerning policewomen.[3] This became necessary to a large extent because of "special" treatment by male supervisors towards female subordinates with regard to duty assignments and discipline.

Conclusion

Female police officers should supervise males as their training, skill and experience call for it. Since private industry has effectively used women supervisors for years, law enforcement should attempt to get more women into supervisory positions as they qualify for them. If women can do the job, then let them do it.

Male supervisors must supervise their female employees as they do their male employees, firmly and fairly. Inconsistent and dual standards of discipline are not good for either the policewoman or the police department. Good supervisors are needed in law enforcement, and one of the goals of police administrators should be to find the best qualified people for supervisory positions, whether males or females.

REFERENCES

1. Catherine Milton, *Women in Policing* (Washington, Police Foundation, 1972), p. 68.
2. Nancy Chodorow, "Being and Doing: A Cross-Cultural Examination of the Socialization of Males and Females," *Woman in Sexist Society*, Vivian Gornick and Barbara K. Moran (Eds.) (New York, Basic Books, Inc., 1971), p. 186.
3. P. Bloch, D. Anderson and P. Gervais, *Policewomen on Patrol*, Vol. I (Washington, Police Foundation, February 1973), pp. 57-59.

CHAPTER 8

OTHER CONSIDERATIONS

IN CHAPTER 4 the main obstacles confronting women in law enforcement were discussed. There are, however, other minor but important things to consider when analyzing the policewoman's situation in America. These considerations, if not examined, could present problems to the unaware police administrator. The areas touched upon in this chapter should be of interest to anyone concerned with the "total picture" of policewomen today. Some things which some readers may want to know about have probably been overlooked or passed over too lightly in this section. For this the author apologizes but feels that some of the really small issues involved in the question of the use of policewomen can be worked out through common sense. For instance, some police administrators resist women in police work because this would mean an added budgetary expense of creating separate locker rooms and toilet facilities in police stations. Another minor consideration is what you call female police: policewomen, female officers or just what? New York City resolved this "pressing" issue by officially banning the terms policemen and policewomen and substituting police officer as the official title of all its sworn personnel.

Uniforms

There is not that much to say concerning the question of uniforms except that female officers must have uniforms if male officers do. Some departments around the country put their male officers in blazers, slacks and "soft nonuniforms," feeling that this creates a less hostile, more positive contact between the officer and citizen. This is fine, and of course, female officers on such departments would also wear "civilian" clothes. But most police departments have their male officers dress in uniforms./If female officers do not have uniforms and males do, then automatically the female's performance is limited in that department./This also reenforces the impression in the public's mind, as well as in the department's, that the female officer is separate and distinct, not a full police officer. So policewomen should have uniforms and wear them on assignments for which policemen would normally wear them.

Uniforms also must be practical. Uniforms for females should be smart, attractive and fit well, just as they should be for male officers. Skirts, handbags and shoes with high heels do not prove utilitarian for female officers assigned to field duties. Slacks, practical footwear and pistols on gun belts must be used by policewomen successfully employed in field jobs./This "controversial" issue has developed on some departments because some feel that slacks and a gun on the hip render women unfeminine. Leaving aside the validity of this sentiment, a female officer encumbered by a skirt, handbag and poor footwear will perform poorly in pursuing people and in physical situations. She will be slower in drawing her weapon from a handbag than if it were on her waist. The Washington, D. C. Police Department resolved the matter by issuing their female officers skirts and slacks. They wear skirts on "inside" and specialized assignments and slacks on field patrol duty. Before a police department decides on a uniform, though, it should consult with its own policewomen or ones on other departments concerning design and practicality of one uniform over another.

Women Police Reserves*

As a former field patrol officer, the author has occasionally been disappointed at the quality of some of the police reserve officers because some definitely fall into the standard, stereotyped "police reserve category." The stereotype follows this line of thinking: "The nonpaid volunteer citizen is often a headache— some join because of wanting to perform community service but others join for 'thrills,' a 'night out,' to have an excuse to wear a police uniform or carry a pistol, or for the 'benefit' derived from carrying an identification card near their driver's license."[1]

*This section was adopted from a commentary prepared by the author for the Missouri Auxiliary and Reserve Police Association, St. Louis, Missouri, April 7, 1973.

But while there are some reserve officers who fill this stereotype, the majority of police reserves are concerned, dedicated community volunteers working for the betterment of the common social well-being of the community.

Before commenting specifically on "women in the police reserves," the author would like to comment on the negative and positive points of the total police reserve program and make a determination as to its value. If the reserve program is of no value, then a discussion of women in the reserves would be meaningless.[2]

Generally, law enforcement today faces a manpower problem. Several pertinent points stand out in looking at the law enforcement agencies throughout the country.

1. Police departments are, on an average, 5 percent below authorized strength and 10 percent below preferred strength.

2. Many communities face increasing crime rates and require new strategies to counteract this additional manpower need.

3. Law enforcement agencies are and will continue to be faced with many nonlaw enforcement functions such as service and order maintenance calls.

4. Advancing techniques and technology require a greater degree of skills in certain specialized areas.

5. Good law enforcement is expensive and governmental finances are stretched thinly because of new demands placed on government by society.

Therefore, the quantity and quality of personnel has to meet necessary standards if in the future there is to be efficient and effective police service to the community. The citizen volunteer offers one definite answer to this problem by aiding the professional police officer. Historically, man began enforcing the rules and mores of his society voluntarily long before he ever thought of specializing and choosing specific individuals to perform these tasks for the community. Somehow, through the course of history, the citizen volunteer has been replaced almost totally by the paid, professional police officer. But various police reserve programs have shown that law enforcement should rediscover the vast amount of community resources that lie untouched. Manpower, equipment and knowledge wait to solve law enforcement's needs for the 1970's.

Up until 1940, hardly any police reserve programs existed in the United States. The advent of World War II forced police departments to shore up their personnel needs by reintroducing the citizen volunteer concept to police work. But several traditional arguments have always been advanced which have successfully impeded and stifled, in many areas, the effective growth of the police reserve concept even to this day.

The first argument against reserves is that police work demands professional, specialized training. This is definite, but many departments do not provide meaningful training to their reserves. They put untrained reserves out in the field and expect them to pick up knowledge as they go along. This is fine, as long as they or fellow officers live long enough to achieve the desired level of training. Secondly, by not having the formal training or experience of a regular police officer, the reserve's actions may bring disgrace to the regulars. Therefore, it behooves local agencies, state law enforcement commissions and reserve organizations themselves to set meaningful and relevant minimum standards for the recruitment, selection and training of reserve officers, as well as regular officers.

An important third argument against reserves is that the utilization of the reserve officers retards the expansion of the regular police departments. This is also a legitimate argument because some communities and politicians have refused to hire adequate numbers of personnel or pay better wages. They have used the reserves as a control lever against the regular officers' demands. This illustrates the total misuse of the police reserves. The reserves should supplement and aid the regular officers, not replace them! Reserve organizations have to resist this misuse of personnel if the reserve concept is to become totally accepted by communities and regular officers.

Finally, perhaps the most important argument directed against the reserves comes from the regular officer. The strong resentment shown by regular officers stems from several fears. Reserves may replace the regulars. Or the officers do not understand what kind of "nut" would do volunteer police work. The main fear of these officers, though, is that the reserve would prove undependable in an emergency situation or more than that—the reserve would prove a distinct liability in a dangerous situation. These often valid fears held by regular officers can be effectively overcome only by relevant preservice, inservice and perhaps specialized training of the reserve officer. The range and lack of consistency in the training of reserve personnel is evidenced by the following: St. Louis has just instituted 160-hour training for police reserve recruits before they go out in the field; the Los Angeles Sheriffs' Department provides its reserve recruits with 330 hours of training and, of course, many departments require no formalized training at all.

After looking at some of the negative arguments against the reserve concept, what about advantages? In briefly looking at the positive points, one easily sees the numerous advantages of a well planned and executed reserve program.

First, the financial benefit that the community gains from non-salaried volunteer personnel allows the agency to put its scarce funds into other programs or allows them to "hold the line" on spending. Supplemental patrol areas relieve regular patrol units to concentrate their efforts in high crime areas. Volunteer personnel can become the partner in one-man patrol units during peak crime hours, thus increasing the officer's safety factor.

A second reason is that during emergencies, additional manpower is often required. Volunteer labor can always be found after a disaster, but *trained* volunteer manpower must be developed and nurtured prior to the emergency if essential public services are to be maintained.

Thirdly, a definite benefit is received from citizen participation in law enforcement functions. Through such programs, many citizens receive an introduction to the field of law enforcement, and eventually some, who may have never considered it, make it a career. Familiarity with the field and the problems faced by the agency create a greater understanding of that agency's needs, policies and daily or long-range problems. This becomes especially valuable at budget time. This also serves the police departments as a screening device, as they provide career information to prospective regular police officers.

A fourth important reason is that reserve peace officers can replace regular officers for other assignments or on their vacations. In a civil disturbance, regular personnel can be concentrated in problem areas, and the security of vacated or outlying areas can be assumed by the reserve. This replacement factor provides an agency with a large measure of operational flexibility.

The fifth reason is one of the most important points in talking about the benefits of a reserve program, and that is the variety of tasks that reserves can be utilized in. Traditionally, reserves have been working almost totally with the uniformed field patrol division, performing such tasks as traffic control, special holiday or "vacation-check" patrols and general patrol duties. While some police reserves wear guns and have police powers of arrest, many do not. Some departments now use their reserve personnel in a variety of tasks, usually allowing the individual to contribute her/his own unique skills and talent to the department in specialized areas. Computer programers, teachers, systems analysts, lawyers, recruitment and personnel executives, guidance counselors and others can all contribute in their own unique way on a volunteer basis in areas outside of field patrol.

And this brings us in a round-about way to the subject of "women police reserves." If departments accept the validity of maximizing the effectiveness of reserve officers by using them in areas outside general patrol, then women should be recruited by police reserve units. In some departments, as much as 50 percent of the total sworn personnel is involved in areas outside of general patrol duties ranging from traffic, vice, intelligence, planning and research to juvenile, police-community relations, training and others.

Less than 2 percent of the entire sworn complement of the police profession are women, whereas women comprise 51 or 52 percent of the total population. Why this lack of women in law enforcement? As we have seen in this book, it is really for many of the same arguments that are advanced against police reserves: lack of training, poor standards of selection and recruitment, regular officers feeling that women constitute a danger and liability on general patrol. Also, many male police administrators were not and are not clear on the utilization of policewomen for a combination of reasons: a lack of knowledge about the effectiveness and the potential utilization of policewomen, the feeling that law enforcement is not "women's work" or the outright prejudicial and discriminatory feelings and actions of the administrator. I might add that no reliable statistics exist on the number of women police reserves and auxiliaries in America today; however, based on observation and limited statistical information from the Police Foundation, women reserve and auxiliary officers comprise no more of a significant percentage than the percentage of regular sworn policewomen.[3]

The only possibly valid argument against the use of women in law enforcement is that on general patrol (even though only about ten or fifteen percent of the officer's tour of duty involves possible physical confrontation), females should not be used. And even this is being experimented within a number of agencies to see if women can possibly handle the rigors of general field patrol. St. Louis County, Los Angeles Sheriff's Department, Peoria, Illinois, Washington, D. C., New York City and other cities use females in one-person patrol units, male-female units or two-person female units on general patrol duties. But New York City Police has utilized unarmed female auxiliary police [synonymous with police reserve—author] on neighborhood patrol duties with male partners for years. Also, approximately thirty women work as a mounted auxiliary police force which patrols parks on horseback. University City, Missouri, employs its female auxiliary police in the same manner as it does male auxiliaries—community relations, special holiday patrol, traffic control and other functions.

Putting aside the general patrol function, though, numerous other tasks exist where muscle is no criteria for the selection of the best person to perform the job. And if reserve officers work in the area outside of general patrol, the women should be considered to occupy these positions, also. The female computer programer, the female juvenile officer, the female detective, the female planner and researcher, the female police community-relations expert can all function interchangeably with male reserves where talent and skills are the criteria. Aside from the various anti-discrimination laws on the books now which might legally force police reserve programs to accept women, police reserve units should want to recruit and meaningfully utilize females because of their versatility.

In summary, the concept of police reserve programs should be advanced throughout the United States. And at the same time talented and concerned female citizen-volunteers should be accepted and encouraged to get involved in the police reserve program. If the police reserves' goal is to aid in the creation of a better community, then citizens of both sexes must strive for this.

Turn-over and Absenteeism

Some employers argue in both the public and private sectors that women workers are not desirable to employ because they have higher turnover rates and a higher degree of absenteeism than males. If this is so, then it should definitely be a legitimate concern for a police administrator who considers the hiring of policewomen.

The higher absenteeism of women workers is a myth, however. The Public Health Service data for 1969 shows that the average man loses 5.9 days from work each year, while the woman loses 5.6 days. This figure for women also includes days lost for pregnancy and childbirth.[4] The Washington, D. C. Police Department's experiment with women in field patrol found that the total number of sick days used by the policewoman and comparative policemen was the same. The pattern of sick leave differed, though, with more females than males taking sick leave, but more males taking extended periods of sick leave than females.[5]

While the female turnover rate in industry is slightly higher than the male rate, "men will resign to get another job almost as often as women will leave for family reasons."[6] But the Women's Bureau points out that the skill level of a job, more than the sex of the job-holder, influences turnover rates.[7] Dull, ill-paid, menial jobs offer little job satisfaction and invite high turnover and absenteeism, and women have a higher percentage of these types of jobs than do men.[8] A new concept in law enforcement is lateral mobility for police officers who wish to transfer from one police department to another. This concept is slowly being adopted in California and the rest of the country. As lateral mobility becomes more widely accepted, police departments will all run the risk of high turnover rates for their male and female officers. But law enforcement will not be losing these officers' skills and training; rather they will just be changing their working environment.

Even the policewoman who gets married and has children is not "lost" to a police department. Looking at the vast amount of data in the 1969 *Handbook of Women Workers* gives a police chief a tentative work profile of such a policewoman. She will join the department for a few years, then quit to raise a family. But even then, if she never returns, she has already given the police department several useful and productive years of work. She will have her last child at about age thirty, and in her mid-thirties when all her children are in school, her family responsibilities considerably decrease. Working mothers of children under eighteen comprise thirty percent of all women in the labor force. If a woman reenters law enforcement at thirty-five years of age, after being out of it for eight to ten years, she still can expect to average another 24 years of work.[9]

Civil Service

The last sentence in the preceding section leads into another minor, but sometimes major, obstacle to policewomen and that is civil service. Police administrators must seek to change unrealistic and invalid civil service requirements. A female sergeant comments about civil service and its effect.

> I think women have a lot of opportunities but quite often they get sidetracked with families and don't spend as many years and hours on their profession as do men. A lot of girls get on and work a few years and find a deputy or a policeman to marry. And, of course, civil service creates a great problem here because you can't be hired after the age of thirty-five and that's when a lot of women are ready to go back into industry. We have one girl here who is a civilian and she would make a great investigator but she is over thirty-five and couldn't even apply. Civil service is really messed up and perhaps you'll write a whole other book on that (6).

A healthy former policewoman wanting to return to law enforcement at age thirty-six who can contribute twenty more effective and productive years to a police department should be hired. Any civil service regulations forbidding this because one is over thirty-five are foolish. As the sergeant noted, civil service would entail a book by itself, but the police chief must examine his local civil service regulations and determine if they prove beneficial to his department. If the regulations act as a hindrance to the recruitment or promotion of useful female or male police officers, then they should be changed. Local civil service regulations should also conform to the various laws which forbid sexual discrimination. Separate male and female hiring and promotional lists should be combined where applicants are seeking the same jobs. Provisions for maternity leave for policewomen must also be created by civil service commissions.

Versatility

We have already touched upon this issue of policewomen versatility in Chapter 4 when discussing the equal pay situation and generalists and specialists in police work. Some male officers feel that policewomen are not as versatile as policemen [since they are only assigned to specialized tasks—author] and therefore should not be getting equal pay with males. While we have discussed the equal pay issue, another question arises about a policewoman's versatility. What is the small police department's need of policewomen? Can a police chief of a small department hire a woman instead of a man to fill a vacancy in his department? Can he feel that a woman is as versatile as a man in law enforcement?

When the question about versatility of women on small law enforcement agencies arose, several policewomen commented to the author:

> Versatility has to be important on a small department and perhaps in the field situations, the male officer is more versatile. But there always will be a job that requires a woman or that requires just the most qualified person and it is there where a policewoman should be used. And women can identify with other women so there should be a policewoman on any size force (20).

> The police chief of a small department sometimes does lose his versatility by placing a female in a position. But there should be two policewomen on any department because of the multitude of tasks she can perform. If you have only one woman officer, you may wind up working her too hard. Say, for instance, that she is working juvenile cases or child molesting but then you get something hot where you might want to use her for undercover or something like that. Or an abortion set-up that you want investigated. If you have just one officer filling all these facets, there is no way she can do it all well. And when the time comes up, things move like one-two-three. You can't sit there and program a certain type of crime to arrive five or six months from now. Or call up and borrow a policewoman from

another department to handle a problem because they might not be available. So policewomen are needed (9).

I feel that law enforcement is three-fourths a man's job. Now if the small department's police chief is short men for the field, there is no reason why he couldn't use a woman as well as he could a man unless he needs someone to patrol at night and that type of thing, but there is no reason why a woman couldn't free a man by doing administrative work or complaint desk or dispatching and jail work. I don't see why if he didn't have any women at all on his force, why he couldn't use several (2).

As versatile? In a small department, I'd have to say "no" because you can't send a woman out alone in a patrol car on patrol. It's an impossibility. You can't have her chasing down robbery suspects by herself and that's just something they would never do, and I don't think they should. On a small department, though, they do have jobs that someone must fill everyday like complaint desk, juvenile bureau, things like that. Now if it came down that everyone else was sick (which of course would never happen) and she was left there, she would not be able to go out in a patrol car so therefore I'd have to say she wouldn't be as versatile on a small department (13).

The preceding policewomen have a point to consider regarding the use of policewomen on a small department. But as they stated, a need exists for people to fill jobs outside of one-person patrol units (if you agree with the idea that women cannot or should not be in a one-person unit), and it is there that policewomen would be effectively employed. The following two policewomen really "hit the nail on the head" concerning the question of versatility:

I would think that a police chief on a small department is going to fill a position and he being the administrator and the chief is going to want the best person for the job. If it happens to be the woman and he has deduced all this down to the two candidates for a job being a man and a woman, if she has the ability to handle it better, I can't see how he could get around not choosing her just because she is a woman . . . Well, women aren't versatile in some things and again, some women do things that the man isn't versatile in, so where do we draw the line? See, there are male and female on this earth and they each have their own role and women handle some things and men handle some things, but they're still a unit, still here all doing the same things, so I figure it would be best if you can work together. Maybe you can specify what their duties and responsibilities are but they're both equal and they're both needed (18).

I have to admit that when a police administrator talks about a number and a budget, he possibly feels that his best expenditure will be in a man. But this again goes back to training and making use of your personnel. If the chief is aware that he has well-trained and qualified women officers, then he should make use of them. You see, the administrator is the key to the use and role of women in law enforcement. If he makes effective use of policewomen, then they are necessary and versatile. But if he doesn't employ them or he tries to save money on hiring a woman officer and instead gets a woman civilian to perform what should be a policewoman's job, then he is quite foolish. I've seen some small departments where the chief will have a woman clerk-typist search a female prisoner. First, he is risking all sorts of liability if the untrained woman is hurt if there is a fight or something; and more importantly, he is putting an untrained woman's life on the line by having her perform a search. All this because he does not want to hire one or two trained and qualified policewomen. Every department should have some policewomen and police chiefs should be aware of this and make use of them instead of trying to find short cuts around hiring them (7).

The last officer makes several good points in her statement. A police chief who tries to cut corners and save money by using a jail matron or a female civilian to perform police work does not face reality. The chief should hire a trained, skilled policewoman for police work and not run the risk of injury or death to unqualified and untrained females by having them perform police tasks. Basically, the question of versatility boils down to the issue of utilization. If male police administrators would fully use policewomen, then they would be versatile. If they do not employ policewomen or utilize them in a limited way, then they are not versatile. Even if a police administrator feels reluctant to have policewomen perform general patrol duties, they can still perform many vital and necessary tasks on a small police department and they can be instantly available for the "special" situations where a female officer is a must. Any size police department should and must have a policewoman in order to increase its effectiveness. One female officer aptly mentioned that "women are versatile in some areas and males in others," but together they comprise just part of one small unit on earth—human beings.

If a police chief of a small department is severely limited by departmental budget and does not feel that a full-time policewoman is essential, he should consider hiring a policewoman on a part-time basis. This will give his department the benefit of a trained and skilled policewoman, and his department will save money by not having to contribute many of the fringe benefits for which a full-time employee is eligible. The policewoman who has quit law enforcement to raise a family may gladly welcome this opportunity to work only twenty or thirty hours per week. She can still take care of her family and earn extra income as well as change her daily routine. This concept can be used by any size police department, as well, so long as any civil service restrictions are ironed out. This would permit law enforcement agencies to retain the skills of a policewoman for several years, even on a part-time basis while she raises her children.

The Media

The media can be a "mixed blessing" to policewomen. The media, of course, includes radio, television, newspapers, books and periodicals. On one hand, the media can expose the public and male police officers to the positive contribution women can make to law enforcement. On the other hand, the media can overexpose the issue of women in police agencies and thereby cause resentment and even fear in the minds of the public and male officer. Chief Andrews of the Peoria (Illinois) Police Department feels that one of the reasons for the success of policewomen functioning in general patrol duties on his department is that there has been relatively little media publicity about it. "It's better that it just happened almost naturally; otherwise, putting women on patrol would have raised a lot of attention and conflict within the community."[10]

The media can definitely affect how male police officers will react to female officers. New female officers are "rookies" and face the same problems of proving themselves as male rookies do. But female rookies face even greater obstacles if the local media has over-stimulated the community about this "great, radical experiment of utilizing women cops." A Peoria policewoman, Marcella Daniels, commented, "I think men would have resented the fact [of policewomen on general patrol—author] if it were written up in the papers and made a big deal over. After all, they have been doing the job for a long time and so if anyone deserves the credit, it's them."[11]

Sex and Romance

Several considerations relating to areas of sex and romance have impeded the expansion of the role of women in policing. Some of the considerations remain subtle and unvoiced, while others are right "out front" and discussed vigorously.

One of the obstacles to putting policewomen on field patrol duty is some administrators' feeling that a woman officer on the street may get raped. What can one answer to that statement except, "yes, it may happen." But more importantly (to the officer concerned), she may get killed. Male officers are killed and injured each year, and there is a possibility that they too could be sexually abused by a homosexual or a sexual deviate criminal. But we train our policemen in self-defense and firearms and hope they are not killed and injured. But, of course, some are. This is all that can be done with female officers as well.

Other police administrators worry that with female officers around the station and in patrol units, there will be some sexual or romantic "goings on" with the male officers. Of course, many policemen's wives have felt this worry, also, and have risen up in jealous indignation in several communities to stop the utilization of policewomen. But again, what can one say about this except to say that, "yes, there will be some sexual and romantic liaisons formed between male and female police officers." This is as natural as Adam and Eve. But several things should be kept in mind about this. Private industry has always had this "problem," and all they have done about it was to insure that an employee accomplish his or her job. How much can one's morality be legislated after work by an employer? And the same holds true for police agencies. The author does not think that with proper supervision and effective job performance there is going to be sexual relations occurring in station house closets or in field patrol vehicles. And of course if it does, it will be because of the mutual consent of both parties involved. This has to be kept in mind by wives and police administrators. It takes "two to tango." The male is just as guilty as the female in letting anything "happen." A male officer who wants or seeks to have extra-marital relations will do so with someone on or off the job. This cannot be prevented by restricting policewomen's role; the wives or police administrators who think it can, delude themselves. Male police officers will approach female officers (and vice versa) with various sexual and/or romantic proposals, and all that will be necessary and given in most cases will be a negative reply. This will suffice, and both parties will continue to perform their jobs without being affected by it.

The wives who have demonstrated against the utilization of policewomen in one-man, one-woman patrol units in such cities as New York, Dallas and New Orleans have not only been motivated by jealousy but also by fear for their husband's safety. These demonstrations might have some longer lasting and farther ranging effects than was initially anticipated, though. Peoria Police anticipated family problems when women were placed with men in general patrol cars, so the chief told the male officers that if any of them would have trouble at home, they did not have to patrol with a woman. In other cities, some female officers on general patrol are married and so have the same problem but from their husbands. This is overcome by not assigning them a permanent partner. Police departments, though, have for too long neglected the police officer's family. The strains placed on police officers have greatly affected his family, and his familial problems affect his job performance. This creates a vicious circle which causes a high divorce rate, a high alcoholism rate, a high suicide rate and a high turnover rate among police officers. If departments are to make inroads against these problems among their officers, they must communicate and consider the police officer's family. Of course policemen's wives are jealous and worried about their husband's safety, but the police department does not tell them anything about the purpose and benefits of utilizing policewomen. The police department has left the officer's family in "the dark" concerning not only policewomen but many other things pertaining to the officer's role. Police departments should institute positive programs to bring the officer's family into the "department family" and not leave them out in the cold where they will be fearful and resistant to change.

Legal Guidelines

The law has been somewhat of an obstacle to policewomen mostly because of its silence. The silence of the law has changed in the last several years, though, affirming the right of women to perform any and all tasks on police agencies and the right to enjoy equal benefits with males for equal work. This section will analyze some of the pertinent legal considerations which apply to women in their relationship with police agencies.

Two main federal laws apply to equal employment rights for women, the 14th Amendment to the U. S. Constitution and Title VII of the 1964 Civil Rights Act. Though the 14th Amendment was passed in 1868 and intended to protect the rights of blacks, it was decided by the U. S. Supreme Court in 1971 in *Reed v. Reed* that the amendment also applies to women. This amendment prohibits states from denying any person due process of law and by its recent interpretation has opened the way for other lower court decisions ruling in favor of equalizing employment rights and opportunities for women.[12]

Equal employment opportunities and regulations are specifically outlined in Title VII of the 1964 Civil Rights Act, which prohibits discrimination because of race, creed, color or sex, in regard to compensation, terms, conditions and privileges of employment by any private employer of twenty-five or more persons. This law, which was amended in March 1972, to include state and local government workers, shows which jobs can and cannot be limited to one sex, in what ways discrimination is prohibited and forbids reprisals against complaints from an employer.[13] As outlined in this law, jobs *may be restricted* to members of one sex only for:

1. Reason of authenticity, for example, actress, actor or model.
2. Morality, for example, restroom attendant or underclothing salesperson.
3. Entertainment, where sex appeal is essential.

A job *cannot be restricted* on the following grounds:

1. Some or most of one sex are unable or unwilling to perform it.
2. Customers or coworkers would prefer a certain sex.
3. The job is traditionally restricted to one sex.
4. The job involves heavy labor, manual dexterity, late hours, overtime or related areas.
5. The job involves travel or travel with members of the opposite sex.
6. Physical facilities for the other sex are not available.
7. The job requires personal characteristics not exclusive to

either sex, for example, charm, tact, aggressiveness.[14]

In all jobs open to both sexes (which would include the position of police officer), all benefits must be the same. Employees are to receive equality in conditions and benefits including recruitment, discharging, recall, promotional opportunities, training, wages, salaries, sick leaves, vacation, overtime, retirement and even coffee breaks.

Finally, a provision of Title VII protects anyone who voices or files a complaint for sex discrimination from reprisals from an employer.

All provisions of Title VII are administered by the U. S. Equal Employment Opportunity Commission (EEOC) which has headquarters in Washington D. C. and various branch offices. A complaint of sexual discrimination will be investigated by the EEOC, and if it is substantiated, the Commission may go to court on behalf of the complainant.

The Law Enforcement Assistance Administration (LEAA), which handles all federal grants to state and local police agencies, also has a guideline based on Title VII prohibiting discrimination against women by police departments. Violators of this regulation may lose their funds or become ineligible for federal assistance money. The Director of the Office of Civil Rights Compliance, Law Enforcement Assistance Administration, hears and handles complaints filed with his office. The withholding of federal grant money by the LEAA or the threat of withholding it will probably have a significant effect on state and local police department policy concerning policewomen, as will the various laws. In two cases brought before LEAA, changes were compelled in local policy because of discrimination against women. In Wichita Falls, Texas, the local ordinance was revised and in Rochester, New York, the police department consented to interpret state law not to exclude women.[15]

Of course, various state laws forbid sexual discrimination on jobs, too. In order to avoid violation of Title VII, the LEAA guidelines and the state laws, many police departments must change their procedures. These departments must begin to experiment by using men and women interchangeably and develop recruitment, selection and promotion standards and tests which are job-rated for men and women.

Under Title VII, police assignments, except for reasons of propriety (body searches), cannot be made only to one sex. Of course, character, size, intelligence, strength, experience and education of the individual person concerned can be taken into account. This decision must be based on actual knowledge of the person and not on a prejudice based on a sexual stereotype. For example, if it can be shown that the characteristics needed for general patrol duty are strength, stamina and aggressiveness, which are normally associated with men but also present to a greater degree in some women than some men, then this assignment cannot be denied all women. This means that women are eligible for any police work including general patrol unless they, as a sex group, prove unfit.[16]

There have been numerous cases which have been brought to court by individual women charging discrimination by police departments which have been decided in favor of the complainants. These cases have ranged from issues of equal pay for equal work to the right to take promotional exams. But basically all the laws and legislative guidelines on the books point to the fact that women cannot be discriminated against by police departments solely on the basis of their sex. It is illegal to deny women equal opportunities and equal benefits in police work. Law enforcement agencies that do so have the burden of proof upon them to prove that "sex is a bonafide occupational qualification necessary to the normal operation of that particular business or enterprise."[17] The next proposed amendment to the Constitution, the Equal Rights Amendment (ERA), should provide the final legal force necessary to end sexual discrimination. It appears that the amendment will be ratified, with thirty-three states having done so already and only five more necessary to ratify it by 1979 in order for it to become the 27th Amendment. Police agencies should not wait for the ERA to become law before taking affirmative action against unfair and illegal employment practices. Police agencies should be obeying the law, not violating it.

Head Administrator

The head administrator of a law enforcement agency has the ultimate responsibility for utilization of females by his agency. The top police administrator usually proves a very strong factor in determining whether or not the policewoman is even hired and, if she is employed, to what extent she is used.

The following policewoman commented on the type of police chief who takes a traditional approach toward policewomen:

> Surprisingly enough this trend in society towards job equality for males and females hasn't influenced our department at all. Our chief of police is set in his ways and he has a feeling and it doesn't seem to matter to him what's going on in the outside world. He feels law enforcement is unique and doesn't take this into consideration. Perhaps he is living in a vacuum. I think his feeling is that women belong at home—period (15).

The police chief referred to by the policewoman does not make sure that policewomen are used to their maximum effectiveness on his department. Of course, the entire blame for the failure to make maximum use of policewomen cannot be placed on him unless the individual department and its reasons for not utilizing women are investigated. There may be a police chief who wants to utilize policewomen more, but somewhere in the bureaucracy of the department, his program gets filtered so that by the time it is implemented, it has lost its effectiveness. Or the police chief may want policewomen, and the city government or other organizations exert pressure and force him to curtail the use of them. Of course, as we have seen, many major and minor obstacles and considerations confront not only policewomen but policemen, the police department and the community when talking about women in law enforcement agencies. The head administrator must be aware of these obstacles and plan to overcome them before they become insurmountable.

Although many pressures face a police chief in introducing or expanding an innovative idea, the top administrator has the ultimate responsibility for the police department and, therefore, must set the tone for it. An innovative, imaginative police chief realizes the potential of policewomen and tries to resist the obstacles placed before him in making effective use of policewomen.

REFERENCES

1. A.C. German, F.D. Day and R.J. Gallati, *Introduction to Law Enforcement and Criminal Justice* (Springfield, Charles C Thomas, 1972), p. 158.

2. An excellent, comprehensive and current look at the police reserve concept in the United States is available in Peter Charles Unsinger, "Volunteerism in Law Enforcement: The Development of Quantity and Quality of Personnel in Reserves and Auxiliary Programs." Doctor of Philosophy Dissertation in Political Science, University of Idaho, 1972.

3. T. Eisenberg, D.A. Kent and C.R. Wall, *Police Personnel Practices in State and Local Governments* (Washington, Police Foundation, December 1973), p. 31.

4. Robin Morgan (Ed.), *Sisterhood Is Powerful* (New York, Random House, 1970), pp. 560-561.

5. P. Bloch, D. Anderson and P. Gervais, *Policewomen on Patrol*, Vol. I (Washington, Police Foundation, 1973), p. 14.

6. Caroline Bird, *Born Female: The High Cost of Keeping Women Down* (New York, David McKay Company, Inc., 1968), p. 84.

7. *1969 Handbook of Women Workers*, Women's Bureau Bulletin 294 (Washington, Government Printing Office, 1969), pp. 76-80.

8. Morgan, *Sisterhood Is Powerful*, p. 560.

9. *1969 Handbook of Women Workers*, pp. 6-9.

10. Catherine Milton, *Women in Policing* (Washington, Police Foundation, 1972), p. 79.

11. Ibid.

12. Milton, *Women in Policing*, pp. 43-45.

13. U. S. Senate Committee on Labor and Public Welfare, *The Equal Employment Opportunity Act of 1972* (Washington, Government Printing Office, 1972), p. 1.

14. U. S. Department of Labor, *Laws on Sex Discrimination in Employment* (Washington, Government Printing Office, 1970), p. 14.

15. Milton, *Women in Policing*, p. 45.

16. Milton, *Women in Policing*, pp. 46-47.

17. *Laws on Sex Discrimination in Employment*, p. 1.

CHAPTER 9

←SUMMARY

WOMEN HAVE PROGRESSED in the field of law enforcement. They have moved historically and in various nations from a position outside the police agencies to varying levels of utilization as policewomen. This change has not come about quickly or easily, however, for the policewoman's progress has been hindered by subtle and not so subtle barriers, largely generated by the traditional beliefs of male police administrators that police work is a man's job and a woman is more suited to do domestic and secretarial work. This resistance to females in law enforcement has left at present no clear-cut, consistent guide as to how to best utilize policewomen (assuming that the police administrator is even interested in policewomen). But today, women are breaking out of their traditional roles and behavior patterns to demand change in their places in society. Policewomen are changing, too. They have proven themselves effective workers in many facets of law enforcement, and they now want an opportunity at promotional advancement and increased usage in police agencies. But there still will be a big difference between what policewomen want and what they get. Their advance will depend on how strong the policewomen are in pursuing their desires, whether or not they deal with progressive police administrators and, of course, how strong resistance is to their progress.

The resistance to policewomen has been quite strong in the past and most likely will continue in the future. The resistance (as noted in Chapter 4) also takes many diverse forms. The public is somewhat resistant to the policewoman because people do not know what or who policewomen are. Quite often, the public image of the "half-masculine woman cop" exists because of insufficient exposure to many policewomen. Another reason for this stereotyped thinking is that many police departments call their clerks and matrons "policewomen," but they have nowhere near the amount of training of a modern policewoman nor, quite often, the professional attitude of a policewomen. But once the public is exposed to and becomes acquainted with policewomen, the response to them has been very positive. As a matter of fact, many of the policewomen spoken to by the author felt that the public would be one of their main supporters in overcoming internal police department resistance toward women. As a woman, she (the policewoman) is seen as a less threatening authority figure and better able to establish understanding with women and juveniles. Also, as a female representative of a police agency, she is less burdened by public resentment of her authority, and, as a woman, she tends to project the social consciousness so essential to police-community dialogue and understanding.[1]

A recent article in a law enforcement journal noted another interesting beneficial characteristic about policewomen. Police-women, on a national average, have achieved a higher educational level than male officers. It has been shown that authoritarianism, a personality characteristic associated with police problems, is not high among policemen who have some form of college. "This would appear to indicate that policewomen do not 'suffer' from the problem of authoritarianism."[2]

Another argument frequently encountered against the use of policewomen is that they are not able to physically handle police work. It is true that women are not usually as strong as men, but this should not preclude their use on police agencies. Women have proven that they can do all the tasks that they have been permitted to do by police administrators. Even if we set aside the question of women in a general patrol situation for a moment, so many tasks outside of patrol must be performed in any police agency. There is no valid reason why policewomen cannot be used in every area and on almost every job where male officers are used. The police administrator must also make sure that he uses his women officers in more than just a clerk capacity. If he does not employ policewomen in valid, worthwhile jobs, he is just wasting their time and skills, as well as the department's money because he could get a civilian clerk at about half the cost of a policewoman. The author thinks that several one-man, one-woman units are valuable to have out in the field even if they are not on general patrol assignment. These units can deal with the increased number of female criminals, as well as the female and juvenile victims of crime. As mentioned earlier in this book, female officers prove very effective on family disturbance calls. Women can and should be used in all facets of police work even in the field. If some police administrators feel that a policewoman would not be effective in a general patrol unit, then they should at least use her in detectives, as an undercover agent, or in specific patrols such as juvenile and sex crimes. The resourceful police chief can exploit the fact that most people today do not think that an "average" looking woman could be a police officer. They can also use her in many of the vital and necessary "inside" (the police station) tasks that are required in a police agency, thereby freeing males for field work.

Concerning the question of placing females on general patrol duty, the proof is in. Females can do the job and do it well. They have proved themselves capable of handling hazardous and dangerous situations as general patrol officers, detectives and undercover agents in various countries around the world. They have also proved themselves here in America where they work on general patrol duty in about eighty communities. Women can handle any degree of preventable violence in police work because attitude and communication skills are often the key factors in forestalling violence in a police-citizen encounter. The amount of strength or the sex of the officer are very faint factors in determining whether violence will occur between a citizen and police officer. And if violence does occur, a properly selected and trained policewoman can handle it. The author does not feel (as some policemen suggest) that a policewoman will use her gun any more or less than male officers. Of course, some times an individual policewoman will not be able to handle a violent situation and she will be forced to use her weapon in self-defense, but this also occurs to individual policemen. Hopefully, unarmed officer self-defense training will be upgraded in this country so that all officers can use their weapons less. Meaningful unarmed self-defense training and baton training are sorely neglected by most police agencies in America.

An important factor in considering the question of where to best utilize policewomen is that not much study or experimentation has been done on this at all.[3] This is one of the main problems in the whole concept of the policewoman. She has been almost ignored by law enforcement. This must end if police administrators want to achieve the maximum efficiency from their personnel. Law enforcement must at least experiment with the policewoman. While some very good experimentation and evaluation studies have taken place in the last several years in America, there still is much more which should be done. Many more definitive studies will be needed before policewomen are accorded full equality in law enforcement. But enough valid, scientific data now exist to permit women to function in police work. Administrators should keep in mind that for years women had been excluded from policing without any scientific evidence that they could not do the job.

The policewoman has already proven her capabilities in various jobs on some departments, but far too many departments employ no policewomen at all. This point concerning the utilization or nonutilization of policewomen relates to the "lack of versatility" and "equal pay" arguments voiced against policewomen. If the police administrator uses policewomen, then they are versatile; but if he does not use them, then they are not versatile and should be getting less pay than males. But the key consideration is that if the male police administrator makes the maximum, effective use of policewomen on his department, women officers will be as versatile as men, and they will deserve equal salary for equal work. Policewomen will not be effective in all areas, though, just as policemen will not be either. But they must work together as a team so that law enforcement can reap the benefits of their work. This teamwork of male and female officers must occur on all size departments. Policewomen are versatile and necessary, and a need exists for their services on any size department in America.

The main obstacle confronting women in law enforcement remains discrimination. Males who have discriminated against policewomen in the past most likely will continue to do so in the future. This discrimination is the real underlying, unvoiced (usually) feeling in most of the arguments advanced against the use of women in police work. The male feels threatened by this "crazy broad" who wants to be a cop. And not only does she want to be a cop, but she wants equal pay with males and promotional opportunities as well. This male resistance then manifests itself in overt discrimination (i.e. no policewomen at all on a department) and subtle discrimination (i.e. the policewomen who cannot be promoted). Former Deputy Commissioner Theresa Melchionne of the New York City Police Department saw the problem quite clearly.

> It is my belief that much of the resistance to the hiring and promotion of policewomen, encountered in the past, is a product of cultural bias. Strongly rooted, traditional concepts of the role and status of women in our society have tended to preclude objective appraisal of the true capabilities of policewomen in the law enforcement field. Rigid views as to their "proper status" have often determined their placement in the organizational structure and have limited the range of their use.[4]

The author feels that Melchionne is overly optimistic when she wrote that resistance toward policewomen was in the past—it is also definitely happening today. While both males and females have been affected by the traditional roles and status of women in today's society, the males have always been the sex with the power and money in America. Now that women are saying, "Hey, let's look at these roles (mostly male-created) for women, and let's change them and redefine them according to what women desire," the man is finding himself caught in change, and he feels threatened by it. This does not imply that male resistance takes the shape of male police administrators or patrolmen plotting together on how to restrict women in law enforcement. This is not it at all. Many individuals in the police field (also in all of society) have been conservatively trained and are reluctant to change and try new ideas and new ways of doing things. Some police administrators say that they want to protect women from the rigors of police work. This throwback to the days of chivalry and knighthood is not true and is usually just a facade for the fact that they, as individuals, do not want to see women advance in law enforcement. Of course when this type of chivalrous attitude occurs down at the street level of policing, then it becomes really dangerous. Overprotectiveness of policewomen is not really beneficial to the women involved nor policemen. A male officer might unnecessarily risk harm or death by being over-protective towards policewomen. If females are to be equals in law enforcement, then they have to stand or fall by themselves. Police administrators and policemen need to be open to change and evaluate and observe what policewomen throughout the world have done and what they can do for their own department.

It should be mentioned that policewomen do not want to take jobs away from policemen. But they do feel that there should be at least fully staffed departments or perhaps added amounts of personnel on all departments to meet the extensive demands being placed on the police. And they want to be part of this influx of personnel in order to assist policemen in the suppression of crime. Some policewomen comment about their hopes for the future role of policewomen.

> The increased equality that women are now achieving with men has already greatly influenced policewomen. Times are changing and more and more jobs and careers are opening up for women in general and policewomen in particular. But we women want to earn our jobs and not have them given to us as some kind of token thing. I think that policewomen have proven their worth and police administrators have realized this and are going to employ more women in their departments (26).

> I want to see policewomen used in a wider variety of capacities and not only in the traditional jail and juvenile areas. Specifically, I want to see more women in supervisory jobs, an area which is sorely lacking now (14).

> Well, I think there will be an effort made to put women into more versatile assignments and in assignments where they've never been before and giving them a chance. I foresee it continuing to utilize us in a lot of different capacities that they haven't tried before (8).

> I would like to see more positions where we (policewomen) can use our brain instead of our brawn in assignments that have traditionally been given to men. Administrative jobs, more detectives and community relations people and just an increase in women all around (18).

These policewomen feel that more women in law enforcement will create better police departments overall. Today, they are needed.

It is difficult to say, though, how the future looks for the policewoman. On the positive side, she is used in more diverse positions than previously known, and she is used on departments where there has never before been a woman officer. In addition, the questioning and probing about women in society today will hopefully cause police administrators and policemen to think more about utilizing policewomen. Many policewomen interviewed by the author felt that the very fact that men and women discussed, questioned, talked and wrote about (i.e. this book) women and their roles and attitudes in life aided the cause of policewomen. And these policewomen did not consider themselves "women's liberationists" by any stretch of the phrase, although the author feels that in their own field and in their own individual ways, they are doing much to "liberate" police agencies from old and traditional thinking.

But many negative bars still confront the policewomen in America. Many "little" obstacles remain in her path. Until recently in California, if a woman police officer was killed in the line of duty, her husband and family would not have received a cash death benefit, whereas a male officer's family would have. Aside from such "little" things, she still remains totally ignored by the majority of police agencies in America. And it seems safe to predict that it will be some time before most of the nation's police agencies will be staffed by significant numbers of policewomen. The best hope for the policewoman's future is the policewoman herself. She must and should join with policewomen around the nation to speak out to try to influence police chiefs and the powers that control police budgets. Police administrators must be "guided" to realize her full potential for the benefit of law enforcement and society. Also, the female police candidate or officer must see that she is treated legally and fairly by law enforcement agencies. If her rights are ignored, then legal action against the concerned agency should be taken.

> Properly educated and orientated, policewomen will make a significant contribution in actual law enforcement, as well as detective work and in implementing positive approaches to police problems.[5]

One of the positive approaches to police problems has slowly been evolving but is used with increased frequency today by police agencies. It is the same reason why policewomen were initially hired in America and that is the prevention of crime. More and more, progressive police administrators, realizing that the punitive approach to crime is not effective in the total picture, turn to many crime preventive ideas and actions to curtail crime and prevent criminal behavior before the law is broken. This will be one of the key areas in the future usage of policewomen and men, also, as police agencies move from the punitive to preventive approach in many areas. A female sergeant comments about this:

> We must remember that the whole gamut of law enforcement and the criminal justice system is going to change. As we get new people with more education, we are going to find out it is going to be more on prevention than after the fact work. Let's begin doing work before the crime and this is where the greater acceptance of women is going to come in. There is going to be greater reliance on sociology and all the humanities—it is going to be a must. And right now society is changing so rapidly. Right now we're not able to grasp the totality of this change because we're right in it. But by the year 2000 you're not going to even have these kinds of differences. Even for your working beat policeman. He is going to be more of an ombudsman, a referral man. You have a problem, I'm going to refer you to that agency, or that agency. And women will be vitally necessary for this (1).

Perlstein, in a recent article in a law enforcement journal, pointed out that a policewoman has a higher educational level than a policeman, and many policewomen have an employment background of working in a "helping" profession (i.e. social work, nursing or teaching). He felt that "she [the policewoman] is the ideal choice to work in the crime prevention and aid to citizens units of a police department."[6] Police administrators must work on preventing actions from becoming a crime, and policewomen could be vital in this effort.

This is another factor which relates to the "women are not versatile" contention held by some police administrators. It has to deal with what the administrator feels constitutes "police work." Many police administrators view a police department as a quasi-military organization. The policeman is seen somewhat like a combatant who mans the "thin blue line" and apprehends the people who break society's law.[7] The policeman is not used enough in a true peace-officer capacity or in the prevention of crime. So the police chief or policeman who holds the punitive approach toward police work may feel that policewomen cannot or should not be used on a police force.

It is the author's hope that law enforcement will move more toward prevention of crime and that the police officer becomes almost as an "ombudsman." But it is the contention of this book and the policewomen who were interviewed that policewomen are necessary and vital and have proven themselves in both the punitive and preventive areas of law enforcement and should be used on all police departments.

Getting more women into law enforcement will not be any instant panacea for the vast problems confronting police in our society today. Police officials and officers cannot and should not expect instant, top performance by every woman who becomes a police officer. This is just absurd. We do not get it or expect it from male rookie officers and females should be no different. And there is going to be the mediocre and below-average policewoman, just as there will be for the policeman. And yes, some policewomen will "freeze up" in a tense situation, some women will be injured or killed in the line of duty and, yes, perhaps even become pregnant. But police officials and officers should resist making generalizations about all policewomen from individual situations involving individual policewomen. Individual policemen also perform poorly at times, and therefore, it behooves the police departments to properly select, train and supervise all officers to the best of the department's ability. This insures that only top-grade candidates become police officers who give top-grade performance on the job.

The first woman entering a department where policewomen have never been employed before will face some problems just because of her uniqueness. The woman and the police officers on the department should be aware of these "trend-setter" problems and generalizations which come into play. As Officer Daniels of Peoria Police points out, "When you are first at anything you have got to be better, and I am afraid if one of the women is just average, it will reflect on all the rest of the women officers."[8] Another policewoman comments on the problems of not having any prior females on a department:

"I think basically that the first woman you get sets the pace. If she proves satisfactory, then you've got it made. If the first hiree doesn't turn out very well, then you're soured and you (the police administrator) don't want to try it again" (15).

So the lack of any successful female role models to emulate will present some problems to the policewoman and in turn her department. But the female can contribute to the betterment of law enforcement, and she should be given the chance to do so.

Women are asking for change in contemporary society. They are not a minority group in numbers, but they have had a minority of the power and status in America. Just as the Negro, Puerto Rican, Indian and other minority groups have demanded their equal and just share of life in America, so, too, women demand it. Law enforcement has realized that it shares the blame for having discriminated against minority group citizens and minority group police officers. Police departments are talking with the various communities and hiring more minority people in police positions so that the police force better represents the people it serves. Police administrators must also take this into consideration concerning women. "Since women compose roughly half of almost all societies, a police force that includes women will be more representative. The use of women in police work thereby fosters democratization."[9]

An interesting aspect of this to note about policewomen and minority group membership is that there is a greater percentage of minority group policewomen in law enforcement than there is of minority group policemen.[10] A police administrator could make his department more representative of his community in terms of sex and minority groups by hiring policewomen. This would tend to bring large numbers of blacks and Chicanos into police work, quickly making the police officers of the community more representative of the people they serve which has several advantages for the community and police department. Introducing new kinds of people (women) into policing also brings new ideas, attitudes and values to law enforcement. This can make a police agency more responsive to the needs of all the people in its community, and it would break down what Chief John Nicholas of Detroit calls "the squadroom set of values," or help in what Chief Bernard Gamire of Miami calls "the humanizing of the policeman."[11]

Policewomen should be and must be utilized in American law enforcement. The author can only conclude this book with the expression of hope that what Former Deputy Commissioner Melchionne wrote in 1967 will become a reality in law enforcement in the near future:

> Today, as never before, police management policies, procedures and attitudes must be prepared to stand the test of objective analysis and evaluation. The progressive law enforcement administrator not only seeks to derive maximum benefit from the mechanical and technological devices available to him, but also strives for the most advantageous use of his personnel. In restructuring the police agency to meet the problems and challenges of our dynamic society, can he really afford to overlook, or under-utilize, so potentially effective a resource as the policewoman?[12]

REFERENCES

1. Theresa M. Melchionne, "Current Status and Problems of Women Police," *The Journal of Criminal Law, Criminology and Police Science*, LVII, (June 1967), p. 258.
2. Gary R. Perlstein, "Certain Characteristics of Policewomen," *Police*, XVI, (January 1972), p. 46.
3. Gary R. Perlstein, "Female Police: The Need for Research," *Police*, XV, (September-October 1970), pp. 62-63.
4. Melchionne, "Current Status and Problems," p. 260.
5. George C. Berkeley, *The Democratic Policeman* (Boston, Beacon Press, 1969), p. 204.
6. Perlstein, "Characteristics," p. 46.
7. J.H. Skolnick, *Justice Without Trial* (New York, John Wiley and Sons, Inc., 1966), pp. 10-12, 237-239.
8. Catherine Milton, *Women in Policing* (Washington, Police Foundation, 1972), p. 79.
9. Berkeley, *Democratic Policeman*, p. 66.
10. T. Eisenberg, D.A. Kent and C.R. Wall, *Police Personnel Practices in State and Local Governments*, p. 60.
11. Milon, *Women in Policing*, p. 38.
12. Melchionne, "Current Status and Problems," p. 260.

BIBLIOGRAPHY

*Aaron, Thomas J.: Policeman and meter maids. *Police, 10*:May-June, 1966, 96.

Anderson, Sgt. Mary A.: *Women in Law Enforcement.* Portland, Metropolitan Press, 1973.

*Becke, Shirley: The first half-century. *The Police Journal (London), 42*: November 1969, 478-482.

*Becke, Shirley: Training of women police as specialists. *The Police Journal (London), 36*:April 1963, 167-170.

Berkeley, George C.: *The Democratic Policeman.* Boston, Beacon Press, 1969.

*Berry, Vareece: Pasadena's (Texas) Policewomen protect school crossings. *Law and Order, 3*:December 1955, 12, 607+.

Bird, Caroline: *Born Female: The High Cost of Keeping Women Down.* New York, David McKay Company, Inc., 1968.

Bloch, Peter, Anderson, Deborah and Gervais, Pamela: *Policewomen on Patrol,* Vol. I. Washington, Police Foundation, 1973.

*Borgenicht, Miriam: Welcome, policewomen. *Parent's Magazine, 20*:November 1945, 34+.

*Boyd, Margaret M.: The role of the policewoman. *The Police Yearbook.* Washington, D. C., International Association of Chiefs of Police, 1953.

*Buwalds, Imra Wann: The policewoman yesterday, today and tomorrow. *Journal of Social Hygiene, 31*:May 1945, 290-293.

*Cameron, G.: Detective Kitty Barry. *Colliers, 134*:November 26, 1954, 32+.

*Carson, Norma B.: Policewomen are an important factor in law enforcement. *FBI Law Enforcement Bulletin, 22*:October 1953, 27-24.

*Chapman, Samuel G.: Waco, Texas—The city with five friendly faces. *Police, 5*:March-April 1961, 13-18.

*Chasen, W.: New York's finest female division. *New York Times Magazine,* November 20, 1955, 26+.

*Clifford, Alice E.: The policewoman in family problems. *The Police Yearbook.* Washington, D. C., International Association of Chiefs of Police, 1959.

*Clifford, Alice E.: The police and family problems. *Police Chief, 25*:December 1958, 44-45.

109

110   *Women in Law Enforcement*

Condor, Stella: *Women on the Beat.* London, Robert Hale, Ltd., 1960.

Cramer, James: *World's Police.* London, Cassell and Company, Ltd., 1964.

*Davenport, John C.: Policewomen serve with success in law enforcement. *FBI Law Enforcement Bulletin,* 27:August 1958, 3-6+.

*Dewhirst, F.: Civilianization. *The Police Journal (London),* 43:January 1970, 38-48.

*Dixon, Lonny: The unusual role of women officers in homicide work. *FBI Law Enforcement Bulletin,* 32:February 1963, 18-19.

*Edwards, Loren E.: *Shoplifting and Shrinkage Protection for Stores.* Springfield, Thomas, 1958.

Eisenberg, Terry, Kent, Deborah Ann and Wall, Charles R.: *Police Personnel Practices in State and Local Governments.* Washington, D. C., Police Foundation, 1973.

Ellman, Edgar S.: *Managing Women in Business.* Waterford, Prentice-Hall, 1963.

*Fagerstrom, Dorothy: Designed for the women in blue. *Law and Order,* 6: August 1958, 60-61.

*Fagerstrom, Dorothy: Make the most of every opportunity. *Law and Order,* 8:November 1960, 54-57.

*Fagerstrom, Dorothy: Practical handbag for policewomen. *Law and Order,* 12:February 1964, 37.

*Fagerstrom, Dorothy: Policewomen's viewpoint on behavioral problems. *Law and Order,* 17:December 1969, 88-95.

*Fagerstrom, Dorothy: Wider horizons for policewomen. *Law and Order,* 18:September 1970, 81-83.

*Folley, Vern L.: Police officer of the issue, Detective Helen B. Sweatt. *Police,* 16:December 1971, 64-65.

*Fowler, Dan: The lady is a cop. *Look,* March 6, 1956, 48-53.

*Frank, S.: Some cops have lovely legs. *Saturday Evening Post,* December 24, 1949, 11-13+.

*Gabower, Genevieve: *Police and Social Workers Cooperate for the Young Delinquent.* Washington, D. C., U. S. Children's Bureau, 1945.

Garmire, Bernard L.: Female officers in the department. *FBI Law Enforcement Bulletin,* June 1974, 11-13.

*Germann, A.C.: Understand your local police. *Police,* 11:January-February 24-27.

Germann, A.C., Day, Frank D. and Gallati, Robert J.: *Introduction to Law Enforcement and Criminal Justice.* Springfield, Thomas, 1972.

*Gibbons, Thomas J.: Policewomen undercover. *Law and Order,* 4:September 1956, 18-19.

*Gibbons, Thomas: Policewoman awards. *Police Chief,* 27:April 1960, 35-36.

*Goffen, William: Civil service law and you: Promotion for policewomen. *The Leader* (Civil Service Paper, New York State), January 3, 1967, 6.

Goodall, Kenneth: The Line. *Psychology Today,* I:April 1972, 27- 114.

Gornick, Vivian and Moran, Barbara K. (Eds.): *Women in Sexist Society.* New York, Basic Books, Inc., 1971.

*Gourley, Douglas G.: *Patrol Administration.* Springfield, Thomas, 1961.

*Graham, Daphne: Civilian women in police forces. *The Police Journal (London)*, 25:July 1952, 217-218.

*Gray, Naomi Swett: Women car checkers prove their worth. *The Police Chief*, 27:December 1960, 10-12.

*Halsey, A., Jr.: Lady cops of the dope squad, Philadelphia. *Saturday Evening Post*, March 30, 1957, 36-7+.

*Harris, Patricia F.: *Policewomen: The Historical Evolution of her Role in the United States.* Unpublished Master of Science Thesis, Michigan State University, 1967.

*Higgins, Lois L.: *Policewomen's Service in the United States.* Unpublished Master of Science Thesis, Loyola University, 1947.

*Higgins, Lois L.: Women police service. *Journal of Criminal Law, Criminology and Police Science*, 41:101-106, 1950.

*Higgins, Lois L.: Historical background of policewomen's service. *Journal of Criminal Law, Criminology and Police Science*, 41:822-833, 1951.

*Higgins, Lois L.: Policewomen are here to stay. *Law Enforcement*, 10:September 1956, 7-11.

*Higgins, Lois L.: The policewomen. *Law and Order*, 6:November 1958, 4.

*Higgins, Lois L.: The policewoman. *Police*, 3:November-December, 1958, 66-69.

*Higgins, Lois L.: Golden anniversary of women in police service. *Law and Order*, 8:August 1960, 4-16.

*Higgins, Lois L.: *Policewoman's Manual.* Springfield, Thomas, 1961.

*Higgins Lois L.: A career in law enforcement for women police. *Police*, 6: May-June 1962, 46-49.

*Higgins, Lois L.: Women in law enforcement. *Law and Order*, 10:August 1962, 18-22.

*Higgins, Lois L.: More about women in law enforcement. *Law and Order*, 10:September 1962, 40-41.

*Higgins, Lois L.: Bombay and a lovely policewoman. *Law and Order*, 12: July 1964, 24.

*Higgins, Lois L.: The feminine force in crime prevention. *The Police Yearbook.* Washington, D. C., International Association of Chiefs of Police, 1958.

*Hilton, Jennifer: *The Gentle Arm of the Law.* Reading, Educational Explorers, 1967.

*Hooker, James E.: *Career Opportunities in Police, Public Administration, Social Services, and Corrections.* Harrisburg, Harrisburg C. C., 1969.

Horne, Peter: *The Role of Women in Law Enforcement.* Unpublished Master's Thesis, California State University at Los Angeles, 1972.

Horne, Peter: The role of women in law enforcement. *Police Chief*, July 1973, p. 60.

Horne, Peter: Women in police reserves. *Law Enforcement*, September-October 1973, p. 21.

*Hughes, Norah: Auxiliary girl cadets—A partial answer to recruiting? *The Police Journal (London)*, 42:April 1969, 181-183.

*Juergensmeyer, Irvin K.: Education for delinquency prevention. *Police*, March-April, 1959, 19.

Kakalik, James and Wildhorn, Sorrel: *The Private Police Industry: Its Nature and Extent*. Washington, Government Printing Office, 1971.

*Kelley, Geraldine A.: Policewomen play important role in Philadelphia, Pennsylvania. *FBI Law Enforcement Bulletin*, 26:November 1957, 3+.

*Kenney, John P. and Pursuit, Dan G.: *Police Work with Juveniles*. Springfield, Thomas, 1954.

*Keyes, Edward: Meet . . . a policewoman. *Cosmopolitan*, November, 1971, 88+.

*Leevy, J. Roy.: The role of the police matron. *Journal of Criminal Law, Criminology and Police Science*, 39:538-540, 1949.

*Lock, Joan: *Lady Policeman*. London, M. Joseph, 1968.

*McCombs, R.: Lady constable: Sis Dickerson polices a tough Texas county. *Life*, September 17, 1945, 19-20+.

*Melchionne, Theresa: Where policewomen are better than men. *American City*, 3:March 1960, 17+.

*Melchionne, Theresa: Role of policewoman in the investigative function. *The Police Yearbook*. Washington, D. C., International Association of Chiefs of Police, 1960.

*Melchionne, Theresa: The role of the policewoman in working with youth, —The bridge between. *Law and Order*, 9:July 1961, 61-64.

*Melchionne, Theresa: Delinquency control programs: Part I. *Law and Order*, 12:April 1964, 46+.

*Melchionne, Theresa: Delinquency control programs: Part II. *Law and Order*, 12:May 1964, 26+.

*Melchionne, Theresa: Delinquency control programs: Part III. *Law and Order*, 12:June 1964, 28.

*Melchionne, Theresa: The policewoman. *The Police Chief*, 33:December 1966, 52.

*Melchionne, Theresa: The current status and problems of women police. *The Police Yearbook*. Washington, D. C., International Association of Chiefs of Police, 1967.

Melchionne, Theresa: Current status and problems of women police. *The Journal of Criminal Law, Criminology and Police Science*, LVIII, June 1967, 257-260.

*Milton, Catherine H.: *Women in Policing*. Washington, D. C., Police Foundation, 1972.

Morgan, Robin (Ed.): *Sisterhood Is Powerful*. New York, Random House, 1970.

*Morman, R.R., *et al*: Multiple relationship between age, education, police experience, and TAV variables correlated to job rating on 101 female deputy sheriffs. *Police, 16*:February 1972, 29-33.

*Murphy, Jack: Motorized meter maids. *Law and Order, 14*:June 1966, 10-11+.

Niederhoffer, Arthur and Blumberg, Abraham S.: (Eds.): *The Ambivalent Force: Perspectives on the Police.* Waltham, Ginn and Company, 1970.

1969 Handbook of Women Workers. Women's Bureau Bulletin 294. Washington, Government Printing Office, 1969.

*O'Connor, John J.: *Opportunities in Law Enforcement.* New York, Vocational Guidance Manuals, 1955.

*Olson, Marilynn G.: Women in police work. *The Police Yearbook.* Washington, D. C., International Association of Chiefs of Police, 1957.

*Owens, James M.: Policewomen in the line. *Police, 3*:September-October 1958, 21-22.

Owings, Chloe: *Women Police.* Montclair, Patterson Smith Publishing Corporation, 1925.

Paleolog, Stanislawa: *The Women Police of Poland.* Westminster, The Association for Moral and Social Hygiene, 1945.

Perlstein, Gary R.: Certain characteristics of policewomen. *Police, XVI:* January 1972, 45-46.

Perlstein, Gary R.: Female police: The need for research. *Police, XV:* September-October 1970, 62-63.

*Perlstein, Gary R.: *An Exploratory Analysis of Certain Characteristics of Policewomen.* Unpublished Doctoral Thesis, Florida State University, 1971.

*Perlstein, Gary R.: Policewomen and policemen: A comparative look. *Police Chief, 39*:March 1972, 72-74.

*Phillips, Wayne: Detective story, female department. *New York Times Magazine*, February 28, 1960, 48-59.

*Pires, A.S.: Word with a Brazilian policewoman: Hilda Macedo. *America, 9*:July 1957, 26-27.

Pitchess, Peter: Startling increase in female criminality. Los Angeles, Los Angeles County Sheriff's Information Bureau, April 20, 1971. Mimeographed.

Pogrebin, Letty Cottin: The working woman. *Ladies' Home Journal*, September 1973, pp. 36, 38.

*Powers, William F.: State policewomen in Massachusetts. *Law and Order, 16*:March 1968, 82-85.

*Purcell, Phillip: Use of policewomen is valuable asset to law enforcement. *FBI Law Enforcement Bulletin, 29*:May 1960, 3-6.

*Rinck, Jane A.: Supervising the juvenile delinquent. *Annals of the American Academy of Political and Social Science*, Philadelphia, 1954, 85.

*Rink, S.E.: Arresting females, the policewomen's story. *Law and Order, 1*: November 1953, 6-7.

*Ronaker, Robert: Role of matrons in detention phase of police work. *FBI Law Enforcement Bulletin*, 27:September 1968, 19-21.

*Rudman, Jack: *Policewomen*. New York, National Learning Corporation, 1969.

*Salzbrenner, Dorothy: Military policewomen. *Law and Order*, 11:February 1963, 36.

Schreiber, Flora R.: *A Job With a Future in Law Enforcement and Related Fields*. New York, Grosset and Dunlap, Inc., 1970.

*Shepherd, Roosevelt E.: *A Study of the Utilization of Policewomen in Large United States Departments*. Unpublished Master of Science Thesis, Michigan State University, 1971.

Sherman, Lewis J.: A psychological view of women in policing. *Journal of Police Science and Administration*, December 1973, pp. 383-394.

Sherman, Lewis J.: Policewomen on Patrol in St. Louis County. Washington, D.C., LEAA Grant No. 3-1008-J, 1974. Mimeographed.

Sherman, Marion and Lewis J.: Bibliography on policewomen: 1945-1972. *Law and Order*, March 1973, pp. 80-83.

*Shpritzer, Felicia: Case for the promotion of policewomen in the city of New York. *Journal of Criminal Law, Criminology and Police Science, 50*: 415-419, 1959.

*Shpritzer, Felicia: A case for the promotion of policewomen in the city of New York. *Police, 5*:July-August 1961, 57-60.

Skolnick, J.H.: *Justice Without Trial*. New York, John Wiley and Sons, Inc., 1966.

*Slack, R.M.: Breaking down barriers: Michigan camp program. *Independent Woman, 35*:June 1956, 14+.

*Slocum, W.L.: *Occupational Careers*. Chicago, Aldine Publishing, 1968.

*Snow, Margaret: Women's role in crime control. *The Police Yearbook*. Washington, D. C., International Association of Chiefs of Police, 1956.

*Sondern, Frederic, Jr.: Crime busters in skirts. *Reader's Digest, 16*:November 1957, 222-225.

Stark, Rodney: *Police Riots*. Waltham, Wadsworth Publishing Company, Inc., 1972.

Stevenson, Gloria: The force of change. *Occupational Outlook Quarterly*, Winter 1972, pp. 11-15.

*Summer, Francis: Lady is a cop. *Look, 20*:March 6, 1956, 48-53.

*Sweeney, Frank A.: The policewoman and crime. *The Police Chief, 26*: January 1959, 28.

*Talney, Ronald G.: Women in law enforcement: An expanded role. *Police, 14*:November-December 1969, 49-51.

*Tenney, Evabel: Women's work in law enforcement. *Journal of Criminal Law, Criminology and Police Science, 44*:239-246, 1953.

The President's Commission on Law Enforcement and Administration of Justice: *Task Force Report: The Police*. Washington, Government Printing Office, 1969.

*Torres, Eugenio C.: Policewomen and crime prevention. *Police Chief, 20:* April 1953, 8+.

*Uhnak, Dorothy: *Policewoman.* New York, Simon and Schuster, 1964.

*United States Federal Security Agency: *Techniques of Law Enforcement in the Use of Policewomen with Special Reference to Social Protection.* Washington, D. C., 1945.

U. S. Department of Labor: *Laws on Sex Discrimination in Employment.* Washington, Government Printing Office, 1970.

U. S. National Advisory Commission on Criminal Justice Standards and Goals: *Report on Police.* Washington, Government Printing Office, 1973.

U. S. Senate Committee on Labor and Public Welfare: *The Equal Employment Opportunity Act of 1972.* Washington, Government Printing Office, 1972.

Unsinger, Peter Charles: *Volunteerism in Law Enforcement: The Development of Quantity and Quality of Personnel in Reserves and Auxiliary Programs.* Unpublished Doctoral Dissertation, University of Idaho, 1972.

Watson, Nelson A. and Walker, Robert N. (Eds.): *Proceedings of Workshop for Policewomen.* Washington, International Association of Chiefs of Police, 1966.

Wells, Alice Stebbins: Reminiscences of a policewoman. *The Police Reporter,* September 1929, pp. 23-28.

*Wells, Alice Stebbins: Policewoman judge number one. *Law and Order, 9:* January 1961, 75-76.

*Wells, B.: Feminine arm of the law. *Independent Woman, 27:*February 1948, 34-36+.

Williams, Carol M.: *The Organization and Practices of Police Women's Divisions in the United States.* Detroit, National Training School of Public Service, 1946.

*Wills, D.E.: Pittsburgh women traffic officers safeguard school children. *American City, 62:*August 1947, 19.

*Wilson, O.W.: *Police Administration.* New York, McGraw-Hill, 1963.

*Wren, Pauline: Auxiliary Girl Cadets in Leeds. *The Police Journal (London) 38:*December 1965, 570-572.

*Wyles, Lilian: *Women at Scotland Yard.* London, Faber and Faber, 1952.

*All of these notations are reprinted with permission of *Law and Order* and Dr. Sherman from *Bibliography on Policewomen: 1945-1972* by Marion and Lewis J. Sherman.

SUBJECT INDEX

emotional reactions, 75, 76
follower concept, 72, 73
general view toward, 68
policewoman's work effective, 40
stereotypes, 68
supervisors,
    problems, 74-75
    training essential, 77
utilization, head administrator's re-
    sponsibility, 95-96
see also Women
Field patrol, *see* General patrol
Financial considerations, small police
    force, 89-90
Firearms use, foreign countries, 57
First patrol duty, 23
Florida, *see* Miami
Foreign countries, policewomen,
    decoy use, 52
    patrol function, 57
    records, 100
    role, 6-16
Foreign experience, general patrol
    work, 57-58
France,
    policewomen, 11, 15
    undercover agents, 57
Future, policewoman's role, 103-105

G

Garmire, Chief Bernard, Miami, Florida
    opinion on policewomen, 24
Geddes Report, policewomen's
    abolishment asked, 7
General patrol,
    definition, 4
    foreign experience, 57-58
    often closed to women, 39
    policewoman's role, 56-70
    see also Patrol duty
Generalists, compared to specialists, 38-41
Georgia, Fort Gordon, women MP
    training, 21
Germany, British-occupied, 8
    see also West Germany
Great Britain,
    general patrol duties, 57
    police reserves, 10
    policewomen's roles, 6-10, 15, 20
    see also England

Guard duties,
    hazards, 62
    women's role, 63-64
Gun, policewoman's use of, 100
Guyana,
    general patrol duties, 57
    policewomen, 12-13

H

Handbook of Women Workers, police-
    woman's profile, 86
Hazardous duties,
    foreign countries, 57
    policewomen,
        abilities, 100
        foreign countries, 57
        women's roles, 62-64
History,
    policewomen in America, 17-29
    policewomen's role, 6-16
Holmes, Clara, English policewoman, 6-7

I

IACP, *see* International Association of
    Chiefs of Police
Illinois State Police, women's role, 22
    see also Chicago and Peoria
Indianapolis, Indiana, policewomen, 23
"Inside" tasks, policewoman's usefulness,
    54, 100
Integration, advantages, 41
Intelligence, role in police work, 64
Intelligence organizations, women
    agents, 17
International Association of Chiefs of
    Police (IACP),
    injuries, fatalities studied, 66-67
    policewomen defined, 30
    policewomen favored, 19
    survey of police departments, 31
International Association of Policewomen,
    functions, 19
    organization, 19
    women officers' support, 7
Investigative work, women's role, 52-53
    see also Detective work
Israel,
    general patrol duties, 57
    policewomen, 14

AUTHOR INDEX